Jacob Kendrick Upton

Money in Politics

Jacob Kendrick Upton

Money in Politics

ISBN/EAN: 9783744723770

Printed in Europe, USA, Canada, Australia, Japan

Cover: Foto ©ninafisch / pixelio.de

More available books at **www.hansebooks.com**

MONEY IN POLITICS

BY

J. K. UPTON

Late Assistant Secretary of the United States Treasury

WITH AN INTRODUCTION
BY
EDWARD ATKINSON

BOSTON
LOTHROP PUBLISHING COMPANY

PREFACE TO FIRST EDITION.

He who said the love of money was the root of all evil spoke not with accuracy of the properties and functions of this commodity. Evils may grow from a love to accumulate wealth in excess, but the love of money is in itself as harmless a diversion as an ill-conceived passion for a steam plough. True money is but one form of wealth, and should not be confounded with wealth as if it were the only form.

He who possesses commodities in excess of his needs for them, and can exchange them for other commodities which he needs, possesses wealth to that extent. In no other way can wealth exist. Money facilitates the exchange of commodities, and, by saving labor and time in the exchange, may give to the commodities a greater value than they would otherwise possess, — only this and nothing more. Wealth can exist without money, and if there were no money in the world, wealth would still remain as before, though perhaps incapable of bringing to its possessor an equal degree of comfort.

The railroad king Vanderbilt may not, and probably does not, handle as much money in a given time as does his grocer, and yet his wealth is reckoned by scores of millions.

In countries where money is not employed, trade is carried on by exchanging direct one commodity for another, of which the following is a simple illustration. A farmer has grain which he does not need, but he needs a pair of shoes, which he has not. To obtain the shoes he is willing to part with a portion of the grain, and if he can find a shoemaker who has the shoes and is willing to part with them for the grain, the exchange can readily be effected. But if, when found, the shoemaker, although he has the shoes, does not want the grain, the farmer will be compelled to find another person who has a commodity which he is willing to part with for the grain, and which the shoemaker will accept in exchange for his shoes. By making this double exchange the farmer obtains the shoes. The grain, however, was in fact exchanged for them, not the interposed commodity. That was used only to facilitate the exchange.

This method of exchanging commodities is called "barter," and to a considerable extent exists in all communities to-day. Prof. Jevons relates that not long since Mademoiselle Zélie, a singer of the Théâtre Lyrique, at Paris, made a professional tour around the world, and gave a concert at the

Society Islands. In exchange for an air from Norma and a few other songs, she was to receive a third part of the receipts. When counted, her share was found to consist of three pigs, twenty-three turkeys, forty-four chickens, five thousand cocoanuts, besides considerable quantities of bananas, lemons and oranges. As the islands contained no commodities which Mademoiselle needed, and for which these products could be exchanged, she must have suffered an embarrassment of riches. These contributions of the animal and vegetable kingdom, transferred to the markets of Paris, would, however, have realized for her handsome returns; but meanwhile the turkeys must be fed and the fruit will decay.

Inconvenience and useless labor have ever attended barter trade, and to avoid them commodities have been sought out and interposed, which, on account of the universal demand for them, will be accepted by any person in exchange for any commodity he possesses and is willing to part with, knowing that in turn he can again in like manner exchange them for any commodity he may need.

Gold and silver have for a long time been employed by civilized communities as such interposed commodities. Neither of these metals, in itself, has any mysterious power. Like grain or a pair of shoes, each is the product of labor, and has a value in exchange for other commodities depending upon the relation to it of demand and supply. This relation, in case of these metals, is believed to be exceptionally uniform and well understood, and therefore either metal can be exchanged for other commodities at well-known rates. Neither metal suffers much, if any, loss from exposure to the elements. Equal weights of either, without regard to form, have precisely equal values, and the relation of value to that of weight in either is such that the amount needed is neither inconveniently heavy nor minute; and the demand for both is universal. For these reasons the two metals named are naturally used in effecting exchanges of commodities, and while performing this duty they are called money. An exchange of a commodity for money, however, but half completes the transaction; to complete it, the money must be again exchanged for the commodity needed.

Bringing money into use, however, the farmer exchanges his grain for money, and then exchanges the money for shoes or any other commodity which he may need. And when the exchanges are fully completed he will have no money left. His wealth will remain, however, represented by the newly-acquired commodities which have taken the place of the grain. The money has gone to do like duty for some one else.

Viewing money, therefore, as operating within

its proper functions, we arrive at certain deductions, which should ever be borne in mind, viz. : —

1. The value of gold or silver, like that of wheat or any other commodity, will depend upon the relation of demand and supply to the metal in question. The miner who takes the metal from the earth exchanges it for other commodities at the best rate he can obtain. If the outlay and labor expended in obtaining the metal will not yield an amount of other commodities equal to, or greater than, an equivalent amount of outlay and labor would yield in other industries, mining operations will be abandoned for other pursuits, until the demand for the metal with the diminished production will increase its exchange rate, so as to render mining operations as profitable as other industries. On the other hand, should the product of mining operations on the whole prove more remunerative than that of other industries, less remunerative industries will be abandoned for mining, until the increased yield of metal will lower the exchange value of it to a point where other industries will be as profitable as mining. In this way the products of our mines are governed by natural forces, and money can have no artificial value.

2. There can be no such thing as "cheap money." In performing its functions, money will be exchanged for other commodities at just such rate as the owner of the other commodities is will-

ing to part with them for it. He can be depended upon not to exchange them at a lower rate than he is obliged to. A decrease in the exchange value of money means a corresponding increase in the value of the commodities for which it is exchanged; otherwise silver would be cheaper money than gold, and copper cheaper than silver, a relation which never has existed and never will. Consequently, in itself, one metal is just as cheap as another for money, and we need select for that purpose only the one which best suits our convenience.

3. Money not being productive wealth, the amount of it in circulation will naturally be just the amount needed to effect the exchanges of products for which it is employed, and no more. It can be used for no other purpose, and everybody will get rid of any excess of it as soon as possible. If by any artificial restraint an excess of it is kept in any community, the owners of commodities therein will not part with them for it except at rates which will compensate them for holding a commodity which, being no longer of use as money, becomes unproductive wealth. Consequently prices of commodities, in such an event, will be higher until the restraint is removed and the surplus money allowed to flow where it is needed.

4. Money will be plenty in localities where commodities are cheapest. A purchaser of grain

in New York notes that for the same amount of money he can procure in exchange therefor more wheat in Milwaukee than in Chicago. He therefore buys in the former market, and sends his money there in exchange for his purchases. Other dealers will do the same, and money will be plenty in Milwaukee and scarce in Chicago, until, on account of the increasing demand, holders will raise the price in Milwaukee until grain can be purchased elsewhere as cheap, or cheaper, than in that market, when the money will flow elsewhere, and prices will again be lower. Money may, therefore, be trusted to flow towards the cheapest market, or where prices are lowest, and to shun the dearest markets, or where prices are highest.

5. A "tight" money market results from too high prices of commodities compared with prices ruling in other localities, and does not result from any lack of money. When prices are lowered, money will flow in. Increasing the amount of money to relieve a market only aggravates the evil it is intended to cure. There being no use for more money, the excess must lie idle as unproductive capital, or at considerable expense be shipped away as bullion like any other commodity.

There is another use for money which has not yet been considered — its use as a standard of value. Gold and silver, possessing a desirable uniformity of value in exchange for other commodities, have long been employed throughout the civilized world as standards by which the exchange value of all other commodities is expressed. The two metals, however, vary from time to time in their respective exchange value as to each other, and consequently but one metal at a time can be considered as a standard of value, without causing confusion. Thus, at a certain date one ounce of gold or sixteen ounces of silver can be exchanged for twenty bushels of wheat; but at another date one ounce of gold may purchase twenty-one bushels of wheat, while sixteen ounces of silver will still purchase but twenty bushels. Whatever causes operate to cause this disparity, it is evident that only confusion of terms can result in attempting to express values at the same time in two standards, having no fixed relations to each other.

If two yardsticks were employed for measuring length neither could be a standard if of different lengths, if of same length there would be need of only one.

Money used simply as an interposed commodity to facilitate exchanges is man's best friend. With noiseless action it takes from him the products of his labor, and in exchange returns to him the products of all lands and climes, and when its work is accomplished modestly withdraws. It asks for no aid in doing its work; no subsidy, no legislation or monetary conferences to regulate its action. All it ever asks is to be let alone. But man will not let it alone! He needs must attempt to regulate it, and so it gets within the domain of legislation, where it does not belong, and brings no end of trouble. Without any excuse, legislation has debased it, substituted inferior commodities for it, interposed artificial barriers to its circulation for the alleged benefit of commerce, and by solemn proclamation declared it to possess a value which it had not.

In no country has there been more interference with the operations of money than in the United States of America. The colonists debauched it, and then drove it from them to make room for unhappy substitutes. Since the adoption of the Constitution, changes in its weight and fineness have twice been made, and one metal has been maintained for years at a fictitious valuation to encourage mining industries, and paper promises to pay have, by law, been declared the equal of the highest rated metal. In consequence of such and other legislation there is afloat a large assortment of money of various values and effect.

Were Mademoiselle Zélie to give a concert to-day in the capital city of this country, its receipts would rival in picturesque confusion those of her concert in the Society Islands. When counted, there would be found gold coin, silver coin, with its three kinds of dollars; nickel coin, bronze coin, copper coins, United States notes, silver certificates, gold certificates, bank notes of two kinds, and perhaps fractional notes,— and all these kinds having a common unit, the dollar, but bearing to each other no necessary relation of value, but all in effect redeemable by the government in gold coin at their face values. Transferred to the Bourse of Paris these several kinds of moneys would also have a value, but it could hardly be computed even by a member of the French Academy. The explanations offered for the existence of these motley issues have been so varied, that few people know or appear to care to know, what the issues are for, or what powers they possess; and so befogged has become the whole subject, that even the Justices of the Supreme Court do not appear to know a dollar when they see it.

The diverse properties which have been given money in this country, the unnatural power with which some of it is legally endowed, and the false position in which other portions of it have been placed, can but bring disturbances sooner or later. Already in the financial horizon ominous clouds appear, and to the practised ear comes the prelude muttering of the brewing storm. As legislation has brought about the threatened disaster, to legislation we must turn for relief. What shall the relief be?

PREFACE TO SECOND EDITION, 1895.

The financial storm foreshadowed in the preface to the first edition burst upon the country in 1893, spreading disaster to every nook and corner of our domain. The expansion of our silver circulation had rapidly increased under the act of 1890. Congress also in that year declared the purpose of the country to be the maintenance of a parity in all forms of money outstanding, thus practically making all silver and certificates or notes issued for silver redeemable in gold, of which there was in the Treasury little except the $100,000,000 reserve accumulated in 1878 to redeem United States notes on and after January 1, 1879. This declaration aroused a suspicion that the reserve would not be sufficient for all the demands against it — and the gold began to disappear from the Treasury. At this juncture the Secretary of the Treasury intimated that the reserve in question would also be used, if necessary, to meet current disbursements. This increased the alarm. Congress was promptly summoned in extra session, and in the fulness of time repealed all authority for the further coinage of the silver dollar, or for the issue of notes or certificates upon silver bullion. Meanwhile more than $500,000,000 of silver had been added to the circulation, worth much less than its face value, but kept at par by the strong arm of the government, which has brought to its aid for the purpose the proceeds of the sale for gold of $162,000,000 of bonds.

The depletion of the Treasury balance is still going on, and possibly other issues of bonds may be required in the near future, and still the inquiry is, " What shall the relief be?"

It is doubtful if permanent relief will be gained except by a change in public policy which will take money entirely from the political arena, leaving other subjects to engage the attention of our legislators, besides the interminable and fruitless wrangle over monetary legislation. Let the country go out of the banking business entirely and devote its energies to more legitimate objects, leaving the supply of money to be regulated by commercial necessities like the production of wheat and corn, — then and not till then will a permanent rest from monetary evils be assured to the citizens of this republic.

TABLE OF CONTENTS.

	PAGE
PREFACE TO FIRST EDITION	iii
PREFACE TO SECOND EDITION	xiii
INTRODUCTION BY EDWARD ATKINSON	xvii

CHAPTER

I.	EARLY COLONIAL MONEY	1
II.	COLONIAL MINTS	8
III.	THE ORIGINAL SILVER DOLLAR	11
IV.	PAPER ISSUES	14
V.	REVOLUTIONARY ISSUES	23
VI.	CUI BONO?	28
VII.	MONEY OF THE CONFEDERATION	33
VIII.	THE MONEY OF THE CONSTITUTION	37
IX.	WILD-CAT CURRENCY	42
X.	THE TREASURY CORNERED	53
XI.	THE SECOND UNITED STATES BANK	60
XII.	UNITED STATES NOTES	67
XIII.	ADDITIONAL ISSUES	90
XIV.	FALLACY OF LEGISLATION	99
XV.	NATIONAL BANK ISSUES	111
XVI.	CONTRACTION	126
XVII.	RESUMPTION	145

CHAPTER		PAGE
XVIII.	THE SUPREME COURT	157
XIX.	GOLD COIN AND CERTIFICATES	171
XX.	THE SILVER DOLLAR	201
XXI.	MONETARY CONFERENCES	235
XXII.	THE TRADE DOLLAR	256
XXIII.	OTHER MONEYS	267
XXIV.	THE PAR OF EXCHANGE	274
XXV.	CONCLUSION	280

INTRODUCTION.

HAVING been requested to write an introduction to the following treatise on "Money in Politics," by J. K. Upton, late Assistant Secretary of the Treasury of the United States, I cheerfully do so because I have found the work to be very thorough and complete, and of the utmost value, both with respect to the history of the past and to the policy of the future.

It gives, in my judgment, the best record of legislation in the United States yet presented in regard to coinage, to legal tender acts, and other matters connected with our financial history.

It shows in the most conclusive manner the futility of all attempts to cause two substances to become, and to remain of the same value or estimation, by acts of legislation.

It gives a true picture of the vast injury to the welfare and to the moral integrity of the people of this country, which ensued from the enactment of the acts of legal tender during the late war, whereby the promise of a dollar was made equal in the discharge of a contract to the dollar itself.

It shows that this mode of collecting a forced loan was the most costly and injurious method of taxation which could have been devised.

It proves in the most conclusive way, the injury which will surely come when by present acts of coinage and of legal tender, our gold coin has been driven from the country, and our standard of value becomes a silver dollar of light weight and of uncertain value.

The reason given for this dangerous interference with the natural laws which control value, and for subjecting the whole business of the country to uncertainty and depression is, that "the silver production of the country must be sustained."

The annual value of the silver product is about $40,000,000 — in gold.

The production of the hen yards of the United States, according to the census statistics, was, in 1879, 456,910,916 dozen eggs, and, if hens have increased in the ratio of population, it is now 500,000,000 dozen, which, at only ten cents a dozen, would exceed the value of the product of the silver mines.

It would be vastly more reasonable for Congress to order the compulsory purchase of two million dollars' worth of eggs per month, "in order to sustain the hen products of the United States," than it is to buy two million dollars' worth of silver; because the eggs could be used, or else would rot, while the silver cannot be used, and is expensive to store and to watch.

This book will prove to the mind of every thinking man that, if we persist much longer in sustaining the acts of coinage and legal tender which now encumber the statute book, our national credit will be impaired and all our working people, whose wages are paid in money, will be subjected to the most injurious form of special taxation which could be devised; it proves that a considerable portion of their wages will be taken from them under due process of law without power of redress on their part, while the rich and astute advocates of the present system will reap wealth which they have not earned by taking from the laborer a part of that which is his rightful due.

It may be said now of the legal tender currency which was issued during the late war, as it was written of the Continental currency of the Revolution. "If it saved the State, it impaired the morality of the people; it polluted the equity of our laws; it injured the fortunes of those who had the most confidence in it; it destroyed respect for the courts;" and although it did not in this most recent case inflict the maximum of injury, as it did in the Revolution, it may yet be said that it did more injury to the material prosperity of the country than all the arms and arts of the enemy combined enabled them to compass. While it destroyed the fortunes of many, it made the few rich richer and the many poor much poorer. Except for its malignant influence the nation would to-day have been substantially free from the burthen of any national debt whatever.

The money cost of the war was a little over four thousand million dollars, measured partly in coin and partly in paper, and it could easily be proved that at least one third part of that cost, or a sum equal to the present national debt, was imposed upon the country by the depreciation of the legal tender notes.

This book, written by one whose official position gave him the clearest insight in respect to the working of the acts of coinage and of legal tender, and also of the banking system of the United States, may be of inestimable value because the chief dangers to which the country is now subjected are the present dangerous statutes still unrepealed, construed under the decision of the Supreme Court of the United States in the last legal tender case, — a decision rendered by judges whose opinions could be predicated upon the political party to which the majority of the court are assumed to belong. It may not, perhaps, be called a partisan decision; but, with hardly an exception, the opinions of the judges in these legal tender cases have been made on party lines.

It is singular that the attention of very few persons is ever drawn to the fact that in international commerce there is no statute of legal tender, and cannot be; hence that all international transactions are settled by the weight of the various metals, chiefly in the pound sterling, which is simply a name for a given number of grains of gold.

It would be very interesting and instructive if some one learned in the law would investigate and explain the first conception of an act of *legal tender*.

Its modern purpose is twofold. First, to perpetuate the evidence that one party to a contract has made an effort to comply with its terms according to his understanding of it. This could be accomplished in many different ways. The second function of a legal tender act is the one which has been perverted by legislation and by the recent decision of the Supreme Court, even to the full extent of a declaration of the court that it is within the power of a legislative body to coin paper into money and to make the promise of a dollar, carrying no obligation for its performance, equal to the coin itself in the discharge of a contract.

This is perhaps the logical outcome of a series of acts of legislation which must have originally been born in fraud and bred in corruption.

This function of an act of legal tender must, in the nature of things, have originated in the act of a despotic power, conceived for the purpose of forcing the acceptance of a debased coinage in the liquidation of debts, in order to steal the property of the people without their knowledge.

I commend this book to the careful study of everyone who takes an interest in honest finance.

EDWARD ATKINSON.

BOSTON, Sept. 25, 1884.

NOTE TO NEW EDITION.

I AM fully content to permit the Introduction which I prepared for the first edition of Mr. Upton's book to stand, feeling that subsequent events down to the present day have entirely justified the forecast which I then made of the evil influence of what were then the present and prospective conditions affecting our monetary system.

EDWARD ATKINSON.

BOSTON, July 25, 1895.

MONEY IN POLITICS.

CHAPTER I.

EARLY COLONIAL MONEY.

The early settlers of this country brought with them from England a considerable amount of silver coin, and, following the practice of the mother country, expressed the values of commodities and kept their accounts in pounds, shillings, pence, and farthings.

It is well known that the standard pound in England was originally a certain bar of silver kept in the Tower, representing a pound in value, as well as a pound in weight. As a pound in value, it was divided into twenty parts, called shillings, the shilling being divided into twelve parts, called pence. As a pound in weight, it was divided into twelve parts, called ounces, each ounce being divided into twenty parts, called pennyweights. A pennyweight was therefore, both in value and weight, $\frac{1}{240}$ part of a pound.

King Edward III., however, being pressed for means to pay his royal debts, directed that a pound of silver should be coined into twenty-two pieces, and declared by royal proclamation that each one of these pieces should be called a shilling, and should be accepted as such in payment of the debts of the crown as well as in payment of private debts. In this way there accrued to the royal revenue two shillings on every pound thus minted; and the royal counsellors imagined that they had discovered a very ingenious method by which a revenue could be obtained without taxation, and without defrauding any one. But as silver, like other commodities, had a certain value of its own, the reduction of the weight of the shilling caused a corresponding increase of prices; and the subjects of the king, finding that through some mysterious agency their property had apparently increased in value, made no complaint of the debasement of their coins.

The successors of Edward III. repeated this robbery again and again, until Queen Elizabeth directed that fifty-eight pieces be coined from the pound sterling, or sixty-two pieces from a pound troy. By this time royalty had reduced the shilling to about one-third of its original value, and yet by edicts and proclamations had made each one of the same power in the payment of debts as the original piece. The shilling had now, however, become so small that the subjects of the queen saw there was cheating somewhere about the board, and they put a stop to any further reduction of the coin.

These shilling pieces were the coins which the early settlers brought to this country.

The history of our currency is little else than a repeated story of the interference of the State with the functions of money, and of abortive efforts to counteract natural monetary laws.

Peag.

New England began the interference. Exploring parties of the Massachusetts colony found living on the shores of Long Island a partially civilized community of Indians. There was among the natives a division of labor: some of them cultivated maize, others fished, others hunted, and a considerable number living along the sea shore were engaged in polishing the shell of the clam and of the periwinkle, which they traded for the products of the field and the chase. The shells were used as ornaments, and had a well-known exchange value for other commodities. One black shell was about equal to two white ones. They were called "Peag," and they answered for money among the simple natives, as did gold and silver among their civilized invaders. There was no limit to the number of these shells which might be produced; their possessors traded them for furs and other articles upon the best terms that could be obtained; and they circulated for several hundred miles inland. Among these Indians, ignorant of the laws governing circulating medium and rates of exchange, the black and white Peag circulated together without the aid of compulsory legislation or monetary conferences. If an Indian sold furs for two fathoms of black Peag no law compelled him to accept in satisfaction of his contract four fathoms of white.

But the white man came, and by statute made Peag a legal tender for twelve pence in payment of debt — and then counterfeited it. Upon thus being made a legal tender these shells became possessed of a new value, and subject to new laws. Lustreless and half-polished shells being worth as much as any for paying debts, a deterioration of Peag at once commenced. In 1648 the Massachusetts colony found it necessary to pass a law which provided that only such Peag as was unbroken and of a good color should pass as money. Peag became so bad, however, notwithstanding the reformatory law, that the following year the colony treasurer was forbidden to take it, and even the inhabitants began to reject it. Again the law came to the rescue and ordered that Peag should be a legal tender for forty shillings — the white at eight, and the black at six for a penny. In this way Peag became clothed with all the legal finery which has ever adorned the currency of civilization. Not only was it a legal tender in payment of debt, but there was a " fixity of value" between the black and the white. Hereafter, if it would not work satisfactorily, the law was not in fault. But Peag was perverse, and, just as great results were expected from it, it wholly disappeared from circulation, leaving the lawmakers to look elsewhere for a circulating medium. They did not look long.

BARTER.

In 1641 the General Court of Massachusetts made corn a legal tender in payment for all debts which should arise after a time prefixed. The exchange rate of corn varied so much that it brought an end to credit transactions — no man being willing to risk future values thereon — and trade was in consequence hampered or broken up. Exchanges, however, necessarily continued to be made, and so a barter currency was established, driving the legally-clothed corn from the circulation.

In 1649, disputes arising about the payment of taxes in this currency, three appraisers were appointed to regulate the values of commodities. Of course if a cow was equivalent to so many shillings of taxes, the lankest of the herd would be proffered for their payment; and consequently the collections of the tax-gatherer comprised an assortment of lean and lank kine, compared with which those in the famous vision of Pharaoh would have been a goodly sight for a county fair. The colonial government was obliged to keep these cows until they could be disposed of in the ordinary course of business. It would be curious, says one writer, to know how much, without giving milk or increasing in weight, a cow thus received for taxes could consume of government rations. To prevent evasion of this sort, in 1658, it was ordered that no man should pay taxes in lank cattle.

The Massachusetts Puritan was not alone in such questionable transactions. As early as 1618, two years before the Puritans arrived in New England, Governor Argale, of the Virginia colony, had ordered that all goods should be sold at an advance of 25 per cent, and tobacco taken in payment at three shillings per pound and no more nor less, on a penalty of three years' servitude to the colony. Notwithstanding this law, in 1623, articles were rated in both corn and tobacco, thus: loaf sugar at 1s. 8d. in corn, or 2s. 6d. in tobacco; and other articles in like manner — excepting the young women shipped from England to become wives to the planters. These last commodities appear to have been invariably rated in tobacco — the price of a wife at first being 100 pounds of tobacco; but the lucky investors must have cornered the market, for the price soon after advanced to

150 pounds — but possibly the increased price was paid in tobacco of damaged quality.

A distinguished writer of that period intimates that it did a man's heart good to see the gallant young Virginians hastening to the water-side when a ship arrived from London, each carrying a bundle of the best tobacco under his arm, and taking back with him a beautiful young wife. But, as even a gallant young Virginian could hardly "hasten" with a hundred and fifty pounds under his arm, it is probable he took along only a small portion of the consideration as an earnest, — thus, in fact, buying his wife upon a margin.

All the colonists were anxious to retain silver as a circulating medium, and their trade with the West Indies brought in considerable silver coin; and the buccaneers spent a good portion of their booty among them. Had no law been enacted making inferior commodities a legal tender, silver would have circulated, being vastly superior in every respect for money.

CHAPTER II.

COLONIAL MINTS.

As another expedient, <u>in 1652,</u> Massachusetts established a mint at Boston and proceeded to coin shillings, sixpences, and threepences; and the law forbade their exportation on penalty of forfeiting all visible estate. On one side of the coin was a tree surrounded by the word "Massachusetts;" and on the other "New England" and the year of our Lord, and the figures XII, VI, or III to denote the denomination. As the right to coin money was a doubtful prerogative of the colonies, the date of 1652 was not changed, though the pieces continued to be coined for thirty years.

The English shilling at that time contained by law twelve pence — it being of such weight that sixty-two of them, $\frac{11}{12}$ fine, would make just one ounce, or 480 grains troy. [The Massachusetts law enacted that the shilling to be coined should contain ten instead of twelve pence, a difference in value of twenty per cent to start with.] But as the mint master kept fifteen pence out of every twenty shillings, as a coinage charge, the value of the new shilling was so reduced that 6s. 7d. of this currency was worth but 5s. 2d. of English sterling, or 22 per cent less, admitting it to be of the weight and fineness required by law.* The English mint, moreover, declared the coin was not of even weight and fineness, and for this reason, in its exchange for sterling, it suffered a reduction of 3 per cent more, thus making it 25 per cent less than sterling. All this was done by the government that the coins might remain in circulation. But they were exported, nevertheless, because there was in existence at that time a cheaper way of paying debts than with even the silver ten pence made by law equal to twelve, and the New England Puritan has an unearned reputation for sagacity if he can be wheedled by any subterfuge into paying more for an article than is necessary.

Nobody was benefited in the least by the coinage of this money. In proportion as the value of the coin was reduced, the merchants raised the coin price of their goods. Confusion in trade and accounts were, however, introduced, and injustice done to many individuals. Then, as now, many believed that a shilling was a shilling so long as it bore the government stamp to that effect, regardless of the amount of silver it con-

* Sumner's History of Currency.

tained; and nobody could understand why the coins did not circulate.

Not to be outdone by the New England Puritan, the Catholic Assembly of Maryland, in 1662, besought the Proprietaries "to take orders for setting up a mint;" and a law was passed for that purpose. The lack of money was assigned as a reason. It was enacted that every shilling should weigh ninepence of English sterling, and that it should be accepted in payment of rent and other debts at its face valuation — thus cheating the creditor out of 25 per cent of his dues. Fraudulent as was this coin, it could not compete in circulation with mouldy tobacco and heated corn, which were running against it as a legal tender; and so it abandoned the struggle and went abroad.

These Catholic legislators, individually, would have scorned to acquire three shillings by stealing or by highway robbery, but they could freely join hands with the Massachusetts Puritans in passing a law to swindle creditors out of their just demands.

These were the only laws for coining money that occur in our history previous to the Revolution; but there was no end to the efforts of the colonies to regulate the value of foreign coin.

CHAPTER III.

THE ORIGINAL SILVER DOLLAR.

Virginia, in 1645, finding that tobacco currency hardly met the convenience of trade, prohibited dealings by barter, and established a Spanish silver piece as the standard currency of that colony, at a valuation of six shillings. This piece, known as the "Spanish pillar dollar," was well received, and, with its halves, quarters, and eighths, became an important coin in the subsequent currency of all the colonies.

This dollar contained at that time $386\frac{7}{8}$ grains of pure silver, and was equal in weight to the pure silver in fifty-four pence sterling. As a sterling pound of twenty shillings contained 240 pence, it was equal to $\frac{240}{54}$, or $4.44\frac{4}{9}$, of these Spanish dollars; and no legislation could change this ratio without changing the weight or fineness of the coin. But Virginia declared there was six shillings in this dollar, and consequently the Virginia pound of twenty shillings could be but $3.33\frac{1}{3}$.

This valuation of the shilling seemed to be sufficiently erroneous and excessive to meet the wants of the New England colonies; and in 1672 they adopted the coin at a like valuation in those colonies.

South Carolina also adopted it, but solemnly declared that a dollar was worth 4s. 8d.— making a pound worth $4\frac{2}{7}$ dollars.

Pennsylvania, New Jersey, and Maryland fell into line, and declared that in this dollar there were 7s. 6d.,— making their pound $2\frac{2}{3}$ dollars. New York and North Carolina said this dollar contained eight shillings— making the pound of those colonies $2\frac{1}{2}$ dollars.

And now imagine to what condition the circulation of the colonies had come, under the various laws enacted to keep coin in circulation, and help the debtor classes avoid paying their just dues. Throughout the colonies the unit of account was the pound sterling, and in pounds, shillings, and pence all values were reckoned. The only money of this kind was the sterling currency of England, and from that country the colonies brought the names of their coins and the unit of account. Had no law interposed, the value of these pieces, as well as their names, would have been retained; and throughout the colonies and the mother country a common currency would have existed.

But the laws stepped in, and, taking a Spanish coin having no possible relation to English money, declared that it contained a certain number of English shillings, which it did not at all, as the law makers well knew. The laws did not even agree as to how many shillings it contained; the shilling in Pennsylvania was larger than that in New York and smaller than that in Virginia. The pound itself had four different values, and none of them that of the English pound, from which it was named. And all this confusion brought about by legislative enactments to force into circulation the Spanish dollar, and to make it do duty as so many shillings.

Notwithstanding these efforts to keep coin at home, Governor Winthrop tells how "traders came to Massachusetts and drained the colonists of their coin."

"The impossibility of a metallic currency in a state of colonial dependence," says the historian Bancroft, "was assumed as undeniable."

The Assembly of Rhode Island subsequently enunciated the following proposition as the basis of the colony's action respecting money:

"This will always be the case with infant colonies that do not raise so much as they consume, either to have no money, or, if they have it, it must be worse than that of their richer neighbors to compel it to stay with them." And this seemed elsewhere to be accepted as a satisfactory explanation of the absence of coin.

CHAPTER IV.

PAPER ISSUES.

The colonies, having exhausted the products of the earth and the shells of the ocean in their efforts to secure a currency without avail, now looked around for other materials. Again they did not look long.

Massachusetts took the initiative. In 1690 an expedition was fitted out against Canada — the spoils to pay the expenses. The soldiers engaged in it returned without any booty, and so the colonies had to foot the bill, as they deserved to. It cost them fifty thousand pounds, Massachusetts currency, of which seven thousand pounds were issued in notes made receivable for taxes. The soldiers disposed of them at one-third discount — according to Sumner — and the next year it was ordered that the bills be received for taxes at an advance of five per cent over coin, with the promise that they should all be redeemed within a year. This kept the paper at par for twenty years, when at last it was redeemed. This was the first issue of paper money by the colonies. It was followed by other issues, keeping the colonists busy as bees regulating the values and trying to counteract the laws of nature.

In Rhode Island issues of paper money were made, not under any pretext that the exigencies of the government required them, but "to advance trade and promote manufactures"; as we hear to-day of the necessity of coining silver to encourage mining industry. The issues, while made in convenient form for circulation, were in the nature of a loan, bore interest at five per cent, and were based upon mortgages of real estate belonging to those to whom the money was advanced.

In 1710, seven thousand pounds were issued, and five years later forty thousand more. In 1721 another issue was made of forty thousand pounds; the interest of which was made payable in flax and hemp, the reason for the issue being the alleged scarcity of specie; and interest was made payable in flax and hemp in order to encourage the growth of those staples.

Here indeed was a shower of wealth, and all who had received the loans clamored for new issues — every new issue depreciating those outstanding, and making payment easier; and outsiders clamored vociferously to get in, on the ground of justice and fair play. But few payments of these loans, however, were made. The legislators themselves were largely interested in the scheme, and consequently the payment of the loans was not urged with vigor. Many of the recipients got as largely in arrears as possible, and then decamped; and the few foreclosures that were made hardly paid for the expenses of the sale.

In 1728, the time of payment for previous loans was extended as a favor to the debtor class; and forty thousand more was issued "on account of the decay of trade and commerce." Other issues rapidly followed, making in all three hundred and twenty thousand four hundred and forty-four pounds. Still flax and hemp were not raised in undue amounts, and trade and commerce were not revived.

In 1751, twenty-five thousand more was issued, the bills " to be printed on new plates." Whether the government thought that impressions from new plates would give additional value to the bills when they came to be used as wall paper, or whether the old plates were worn out, does not appear. All these bills were declared by law to be equivalent to a certain amount of silver, but they passed in circulation at entirely different rates. For some reason these bills came to be called "old tenor" and "new tenor"; and the last named was declared to be equal to silver at 6s. 9d. sterling per ounce, and this was to be equal to 13s. 6d. new tenor, or 54s. old tenor.

In 1763, Parliament prohibited the colonial

issue of legal tender paper, and the courts arbitrarily fixed the scale of depreciation for settlement of debts. One Spanish dollar was to be equivalent to seven pounds old tenor notes.

In 1764 the rate of old tenor bills was fixed at one to twenty-three and a third; in 1769 six shillings lawful money was to be reckoned equal to eight pounds old tenor. In 1770 old tenor notes were no longer allowed to circulate, and these with the new tenor soon disappeared entirely. Thus did the vision of wealth dissipate.

Rhode Island had enjoyed more than any other colony a prosperous trade with the West Indies, which had brought much wealth, especially to the merchants of Newport. In her sister colony, however, paper money had been superseded by silver coin, and the foreign trade, which bounties could not revive or retain, left Newport for Boston, never to return.

In 1709, New Hampshire, Rhode Island, Connecticut, New York, and New Jersey joined in an expedition against Canada, and issued bills of credit to meet the expenses, making them a legal tender in payment of debt. After considerable depreciation these notes were redeemed at different rates.

Pennsylvania, in 1723, issued bills of credit, but on such terms as was thought would prevent their depreciation. Imitating the policy of Rhode

Island, it loaned the bills upon land security, but in addition thereto also loaned upon plate deposited in the Loan Office, obliging borrowers to pay five per cent interest. The loan was for sixteen years, payable one-sixteenth annually.

Franklin heartily approved the scheme, and printed a pamphlet in favor of it. In his autobiography he hints at his reason for his interest in the emission: "My friends there, who thought I had been of some service, thought fit to reward me by employing me in printing the money — a very profitable job, and a great help to me." Later on, he still argued the emission to be a good thing. but thought probably they had enough of it.

These bills were perhaps better than those issued by other colonies; but notwithstanding the security on which they were issued, soon depreciated to one hundred and ninety of bills to one hundred of sterling.

Connecticut also issued legal tender bills for the expenses of the government, but not as a loan. For a time the issue was prudently managed, but the voluminous circulation of the other colonies overcame the restraint, and depreciation followed. Between 1744 and 1746 the enormous amount of one hundred and thirty-one thousand pounds was issued, and one ounce of silver became worth sixty shillings in paper.

The historian Bronson says: "This last emission broke the camel's back. . . . . Trade was embarrassed, and the utmost confusion prevailed. No safe estimate could be made as to the future, and credit was almost at an end. No man could safely enter into a contract which was to be discharged in money at a subsequent date. Prudence and sagacity in the management of business were without their customary reward."

In 1751 Parliament prohibited the colonies of Rhode Island, Connecticut, Massachusetts, and New Hampshire from issuing any more bills of credit, or to reissue those already out. But the prohibition was not to operate in cases of extraordinary emergencies, or in case of invasion, but in no case were the bills to be a legal tender.

Subsequently, however, between October, 1771, and October, 1774, Connecticut issued thirty-nine thousand pounds in bills of credit, bearing no interest, but reasonable and sufficient taxes to meet their redemption were levied, and they did not depreciate.

In the emission of paper all the other colonies took part, and with substantially like results.

One after another the paper issues disappeared from circulation, and the colonies were generally free from irredeemable currency before the outbreak of the war of the Revolution.

So disastrous to business and so repulsive to the consciences of all men of probity were these issues that all parties became loud in their condemnation. A fervent but observant French author, writing at the time, gives a clear impression of the condition of society at that period: "This State is ravaged by a political scourge, more terrible than either mosquitoes or fever; it is called paper money. . . . . It gives birth to an infamous kind of traffic — that of buying and selling it by deceiving the ignorant; a commerce which discourages industry, corrupts the morals, and is a great detriment to the public. . . . . Patriotism is consequently at an end, cultivation languishes, and commerce declines."

Massachusetts had led the colonies into this financial bog; and also led the way out of it.

The depreciation of the paper of this colony had decreased in 1741 to five hundred and fifty to one. About that time, the governor of that colony took it into his head to capture Louisburg from the French. There seems to have been no provocation at all for this action. It was purely a freebooting expedition — but popular with the masses, and it was successful. To pay expenses additional issues of paper money were made, and so rapidly did they depreciate that in 1749 they were quoted at eleven hundred to one.

The Parliament of the mother country, however, was greatly annoyed at the action of Massachusetts in capturing Louisburg, and voted to redeem it from the colonies by paying a handsome sum. Of this amount Massachusetts received one hundred and thirty-eight thousand six hundred and forty-nine pounds sterling; and with it redeemed all her paper issues at eleven to one, and still had a goodly sum left.

Double Standard.

The paper issues of the Massachusetts colony being out of the way, silver coin appeared to take their place. As the issues of the other colonies disappeared, the circulation of this coin became more and more general. Even some gold was found daringly attempting to circulate among these financial robbers. It could not escape the vigilant eye of the General Court of Massachusetts, a Court which has ever been on the alert to provide a law to regulate all human actions.

With the declared purpose to facilitate trade, this Court, in 1762, made gold a legal tender at $2\frac{1}{2}$d. per grain, reducing the existing standard about five per cent. At this rating, debts could be paid cheaper in gold than in silver, and so the silver coins went out of the country, leaving gold to circulate alone. The silver, however, did not leave without returns in exchange therefor. These returns consisted mainly of manufactured goods, and needlessly expensive wares.

The disappearance of silver could not be accounted for; but was believed by the Court to be due to the extravagance of the people, as shown by their excessive importation of foreign goods. It was therefore resolved by a large class of people that, until times were better and money less scarce, they would wear no article of foreign manufacture — a panacea for evils of this kind, which has not been restricted to the last century, or to the colony of Massachusetts Bay.

This was the first effort in America to establish a double standard of values. It resulted, as have all such efforts, in retaining the metal overrated in value, and driving the other from circulation. The scarcity of silver led to the agitation of the issue of more paper money, but without immediate success.

CHAPTER V.

REVOLUTIONARY ISSUES.

MEANWHILE events were shaping for a radical change in the political organization of the colonies. The mother country, owing to her incessant wars with France, was pressed for means, and as considerable expense had been incurred from time to time in protecting her American possessions from the invasion of the French and Indians, her Parliament levied a tax on the colonies to obtain the repayment in part of such expenditures. Against this policy there was a stout resistance on the part of the colonies, which had not before been subjected to a direct tax of the kind, in view of which Parliament receded from all its purposes, except to impose a tax of twopence a pound on tea; and as an export duty of considerably more than that amount on the articles shipped from England to the colonies had just been taken off, the colonies could have no especial cause of complaint as to the amount of the tax. They appeared to be willing to recognize the right of England to impose an export duty upon any articles shipped to them and also to forbid their trading directly with other nations. Such restrictions were considered as necessary to regulate trade, but to impose a direct tax was an indignity which they would not tolerate. A cry was therefore raised of "no taxation without representation"—a principle in political economy which did not exist in the colonies themselves, did not exist in the mother country, in fact never did and probably never will in reality exist in any political community. But it proved a powerful rallying cry, and Dec. 16, 1773, three cargoes of tea from England, ready to be landed in Boston, were thrown overboard in the harbor; and war was inevitable. Delegates from the several colonies united promptly in forming what was called the "Continental Congress."

On the 19th of April, 1775, a conflict of arms occurred at Lexington, Massachusetts; and so prompt was this Congress, not only in organizing its armies to meet the invading foe, but also in providing means for carrying on the war, that before the end of that month it had issued two million dollars of Continental bills, in effect legal tender in the payment of debt.

If ever the issue of paper money can be justified, the action of Congress in this matter should not be censured. A large portion—probably a majority—of the people of the several colonies had inaugurated the war, to which they subsequently pledged their lives, fortune, and sacred honor, and were earnest in its prosecution. Unfortunately they had not given to Congress the power to levy taxes to meet expenses. Congress therefore could not, and the colonies would not, levy a tax to support the war; and there was no other alternative for Congress but to issue these bills or to abandon the contest.

For a time the bills floated at par with coin, and to the colonies the first instalment of paper was as if some one had given them two million silver dollars. The urgent necessity for means was thus temporarily bridged over; and the plan of issuing bills seemed so easy a method of obtaining revenue, that all propositions for taxation were abandoned; and other issues of bills rapidly followed. By the end of the year they amounted to $19,000,000. Before that time, however, the coin had left the country, and the bills were depreciated considerably below par in specie.

Congress implored the colonies in the most fervent manner to impose a tax to carry on the war; but the colonies, familiar with the issue of notes, and having before them the apparently successful policy of Congress in issuing them, took no steps towards taxation; but, instead, commenced issuing bills of their own — amounting in 1775 to nearly $3,000,000, of which Virginia issued $875,000.

The policy of no taxation, and of issuing bills

of credit, was now thoroughly established; and each colony, fearing some other one might secure an advantage, hastened to put in circulation the greatest possible amount of bills in the least possible time. Congress also kept its presses running with such rapidity that bills were issued considerably in excess of the amount authorized, before the machine could be stopped, putting into circulation in the course of five years about $241,000,000. The several colonies found, when counted, that they had issued meanwhile, of their own bills, an additional amount of over $210,000,000.

The Continental currency continued to depreciate, as the issues continued to be made, but the emissions authorized during 1778 amounted to about $63,500,000. In December of that year Congress published an address to the people, in which it said: " We should pay an ill compliment to the understanding and honor of every true American, were we to adduce many arguments to show the baseness or bad policy of violating our national faith, or omitting to pursue the measures necessary to preserve it. A bankrupt, faithless republic would be an invalid in the political world. . . . Apprised of this consequence, knowing the value of national character, and impressed with a due sense of the immutable laws of justice and honor, it is impossible that Americans should think without horror of such an execrable deed."

The emissions of 1779, however, amounted to $140,000,000, having a coin value, according to Mr. Jefferson, of nearly $7,329,278.

In March, 1780, this same Congress authorized silver to be received for paper at the rate of one to 140, forgetful of all its brave words; and also provided for the redemption of the money in certificates which seemed to be equally worthless. This action did not check the depreciation of the currency, but notwithstanding the depreciation it continued to circulate north of the Potomac until the end of 1780. "In Virginia and North Carolina," says Mr. Jefferson, "it continued a year longer, and then expired without a groan;" or as Dr. Bronson says, with a pathos very touching, "it gently fell asleep in the hands of its last possessor."

CHAPTER VI.

CUI BONO?

The country being now practically without a circulating medium, Congress was at its wits' end to provide one. But, while Congress hesitated, silver coin came into circulation as if by magic. This might have been expected; in fact there never was any good reason for its disappearance from the country. The privateers fitted out by the colonies brought into our ports valuable prizes, adding great wealth to the merchants in our cities. The farmers in the country found in the British army a ready purchaser for all surplus products of their farms at enhanced prices, for which they received coin, and as soon as the channels of trade were relieved of paper money, specie naturally and readily took its place, although Cornwallis had not surrendered, and independence was far from being achieved.

The expenses of the war from that time onward were met by the proceeds of loans obtained in France and Holland, which were successfully negotiated and honorably paid at maturity.

Throughout all the struggle there is evidence of but little, if any, revenue having been raised by direct taxation. Paper money and other forms of indebtedness, together with the $10,000,000 of coin received from foreign loans, constituted the entire resources of the colonies with which they conducted the War of Independence to a successful termination.

But the issue of the paper money, and its subsequent practical repudiation, <u>was in effect a tax levied upon the people equal to its value in specie at the time of its emission</u>. This value has been estimated by Jefferson at about $74,000,000. And who paid this sum? As the notes gradually became of less and less value, each holder of them suffered a tax equivalent to the amount of their depreciation while in his hands. Thus, if a person received $1,000 of notes equivalent at the time to $900 in specie, and, retaining them in his hands in the meantime, afterwards paid them out when worth but $800 in specie, he paid a tax to the government in the transaction of $100.

This method of imposing a tax could hardly be outdone in the injustice of its operation. The patriotic men who sympathized with the little band struggling for independence, and the soldiers who fought the battles, took the money as a patriotic duty, trying as best they knew to maintain its value. It was in their hands mainly that the depreciation occurred, and by them that the loss was suffered. The speculator, the camp follower, and the tory, either refused it altogether, or took it and disposed of it at such a rate as to secure a profit.

If, instead of issuing this money, a tax had been levied by the colonies mainly upon the property of the country, the exaction would have fallen where it could have been easily borne.

In truth, the wealth of the country had but little sympathy with the men who projected or were carrying on the war of the rebellion. The Hon. Charles Biddle, one of the foremost men of the time, a friend of Franklin, and thoroughly in sympathy with the war, who says, in his recently published autobiography, that as a young man he was present at the State House in Philadelphia on the fourth of July, 1776, when the Declaration of Independence was read, relates that a large share of the intelligence and nearly all the wealth of Philadelphia was enlisted on the side of the mother country, and that nearly half of the people and nearly all the wealthy citizens of New York city were in like sympathy.

Their objection to the war was based upon what they believed to be patriotic feeling. Even in case of success they feared the colonies would not be able to unite in one nation; but would be broken into thirteen States, without any standing among the nations of the earth, and without ability to maintain their own independence.

Recognizing, as we must, their sincerity of purpose and the strong reasons they gave for sympathizing with the mother country, there still remains the fact that a majority of the colonists were struggling for independence, and that they had the right to tax the wealth of the land to aid them in their cause, even if they could not command personal aid and sympathy from its owners.

Had it not been for the adoption of paper money, there would have been no recourse for the colonists but taxation, and with a tax levy judiciously planned, and courageously enforced, the war could not have lasted long, and the horrors of Valley Forge would have been unknown.

As it was, the patriotic men, drawn largely from the lower walks of life, not only achieved for us our independence, but, through their unnecessary deprivation, met by far the larger part of the expenses of the conflict borne by that generation. So far as the necessity of providing a circulation was concerned, this policy was certainly uncalled for. The fact that, long before the war was over, there was an abundance of silver in circulation clearly indicates that at no time, with a proper financial policy, would the colonists have been embarrassed for the want of a sound circulating medium.

Of the ability of the colonies to have met by taxation the expenses of the war, there can be little doubt. Mr. Jefferson estimates that the entire cost of the eight years of war was $140,000,000 in specie. Deducting therefrom $10,000,000 obtained through foreign loans, and we find that to have met the annual expense of the war by taxation would have required but about $16,000,000. The population of the colonies at that time was not less than 3,000,000, and consequently a tax each year equivalent to the rate of $5.25 per capita, levied upon property and rigorously collected, would have met the entire payment of the war expenses; and any hardships attending its payment would have been thrown upon the wealth of the country, which so largely failed to lend a helping hand. This rate of taxation cannot be considered excessive. The country has been subjected since to a greater rate of taxation. During the four years following our late civil war, the government collected an equivalent of about $360,000,000 per annum in specie; equivalent to a per capita tax of about $8.25, and yet no especial hardships resulted.

But the colonists, with a mistaken financial policy, no more hesitated to challenge the law of nature than to meet the forces of George III. Victorious as they were over the forces of his most powerful Majesty, they were unable to resist the silent but ever present force which ultimately sent their paper dollars to the waste basket.

CHAPTER VII.

MONEY OF THE CONFEDERATION.

The Continental Congress continued its session after the close of the war, but indulged in few experiments with paper money, though propositions for further emissions were agitated in several of the colonies.

In 1781 Congress instructed the Superintendent of Finance, Robert Morris, to report to it a table of rates at which the different foreign coins should be received at the public treasury. This information was important and necessary, as the country had yet no coinage of its own, and the relations of the several foreign coins were not well understood, except among dealers in bullion.

Morris promptly replied to the resolution, but gave none of the information asked for, stating, however, that the resolution suggested to him something else: and that was, the various standards of values existing throughout the colonies; and after discussing at length the lamentable confusion resulting therefrom, he recommended that a mint be established for a new and uniform coinage, expressed in the terms of a unit of value, which should be fixed by law.

Several months later he further replied to Congress, again recommending the establishment of a mint; meanwhile all foreign coins to be received according to their weight and fineness, their values to be expressed in the terms of dollars, of which values he submitted an estimate. "I take," he says, "the liberty to observe that this estimation of coins is founded upon the quantity of alloy which they respectively contain."

On Feb. 21, 1782, Congress approved of his suggestion to establish a mint; and directed him to report a plan for conducting the institution.

In compliance therewith, he recommended the adoption of the Spanish dollar, containing, as he believed, three hundred and seventy-three grains of pure silver, as a standard; and thought it would be necessary to divide it into one thousand four hundred and forty parts, so that the pennies of the several States might find therein an exact expression of their respective values. He proposed two copper coins, one containing eight and the other five of these units. The silver value of the unit would be one-fourth of a grain. Proceeding decimally, one hundred would be twenty-five grains, which was to be the lowest of the silver coins; "and this might be," he says, "called a cent;" but he gives no reason for this possible nomenclature. Probably from these crude and impracticable suggestions was evolved our decimal currency, based upon the standard proposed — the Spanish silver dollar, though this coin was subsequently reduced in weight.

In 1785, the Congress of the confederation adopted this coin as the ideal unit of value; and the following year decided that it contained 375.64 grains of pure silver. The amount of silver contained in this piece had before been subjected to reductions. In 1707 this dollar was declared by the English mint to contain $386\frac{7}{8}$ grains; and in 1772 the amount of pure silver in it had been fixed by law at $377\frac{1}{4}$ grains. Probably the coins upon which Morris based his estimate had been some time in circulation and were somewhat worn by use.

The same act which fixed the value of the dollar provided for a decimal subdivision in coins, and for the coinage of the dime (10c.), double-dime (20c.) and half dollar (50c.) containing proper proportions of silver. The policy of establishing a decimal currency in this country was by this act authoritatively determined upon.

The same enactment authorized the coinage of the gold eagle, containing 246.268 grains of fine gold, and a half eagle of proportionate weight of the same fineness, and also of the copper cent and half-cent. These subdivisions of the dollar were probably due to suggestions of Mr. Jefferson, whose memorandum, without date, contains recommendations to that effect. The ratio of gold and silver in these coins, it will be seen, was 1 to 15.253, while the market valuation of the two metals was 1 to 14.89. The reason for thus undervaluing silver coin cannot at this day be ascertained. Silver had always been relied upon for currency throughout the colonies; but undervalued, as provided in this enactment, it would soon have disappeared from circulation.

The same Congress also authorized a mint, and the accounts of Mr. Morris show that he expended about $2,000 thereon, and prepared a few dies for the copper coins; but no coins were issued. The confederation, however, was making way for the establishment of the present form of government, and the coinage act was of no effect.

CHAPTER VIII.

THE MONEY OF THE CONSTITUTION.

In 1787 the Constitution was framed. It provided that no State should coin money, emit bills of credit, or make anything but gold or silver coin a tender in payment of debt; also that Congress should have power to coin money and regulate the value thereof. In framing this document a proposition was made to give Congress power to emit bills of credit, but it received only two votes. Evidently the delegates had too fresh a recollection of the appalling results which had followed the issue of bills under the confederation; and standing on the wreck of more than four hundred millions of paper money they had little sympathy with any proposition for further experiments of the same kind. There can be no doubt that the framers of the constitution contemplated only a hard money currency for the future of this country.

The constitution was adopted in 1789, and Congress, in its first session thereunder, declared that the treasury should receive only coin in payment of public dues, and fixed the rates at which such coin should be received.

Mr. Hamilton was made Secretary of the Treasury, and in response to a resolution of the House of Representatives, in May, 1791, he transmitted to that body his plan for the establishment of a mint, submitting therewith an exhaustive discussion of the policy to be pursued in future coinage operations.

The pound was still the unit of account, though of different values in the several States, but it was not easy to say what was the unit of coins. In adjusting foreign exchanges, preference appears to have been given the silver dollar, but even this piece had no well-determined weight or fineness. Changes in it, as before stated, had been made from time to time, and the value of any one piece depended, therefore, somewhat on the date of its coinage. There was also in circulation the Seville dollar of 386 grains, in which many contracts pertaining to land were understood to have been made. A reform of the currency seemed absolutely necessary, and, after much discussion, Hamilton concluded that the unit in the coins of the United States ought to correspond with $24\frac{3}{4}$ grains of pure gold, and $371\frac{1}{4}$ grains of pure silver, each answering to a dollar in the money of accounts.

As the principal difficulty in the existing coinage was, he admitted, the presence of three or four coins each bearing the name of a dollar, but of a different weight and fineness, it seems strange that he should have attempted to cure this evil by proposing the issue of two more dollars, the silver one in weight unlike that of any already existing, and the gold one bearing a relation in weight of 1 to 15 to that of silver; thus giving the country two more dollars to select from in computing their exchanges and keeping their accounts.

Congress, however, acted upon his suggestion and authorized a mint, and the coinage of gold and silver pieces with the relation recommended. This act was approved April 2, 1792, and few acts more far-reaching in effect have ever found place upon our statute books. Upon it, thereafter, were to depend the relation of debtor and creditor, the expressed values of property, and all the intricate relations of prices and labor which were to be thereby influenced, beneficially or otherwise.

He admitted that if the ratio between the metals should not prove to be the commercial one, there was hope of retaining only the overvalued metal in circulation. He asserted his belief, however, that 1 to 15 would prove to be the commercial ratio which for a time closely approximated thereto, but in the years immediately following the market ratio steadily increased, one pound of gold becoming worth $15\frac{1}{4}$ pounds of silver. Consequently silver was worth more at the mint than in the market and the silver dollar became the unit of account and the standard of value, which place it held until 1834.

It seems almost a discredit to the genius of Hamilton to believe that he thought gold would circulate while thus erroneously valued. History was full of precedents to the contrary, and the selfishness of man, which leads him to seek the cheaper of two commodities with which to pay his debts, can be relied upon as a constant factor in problems of this kind.

In the absence of gold from our circulation, silver could not be expected to meet all the requirements of commercial transactions in a rapidly growing country. Some method of making exchanges involving large amounts was necessary, and, whatever may have been the mistakes of Hamilton in computing the metallic ratio, he certainly did not lack foresight in anticipating the difficulties likely to arise from the need of a less cumbersome medium than silver coin. In December, 1790, he had recommended to Congress the establishment of a national bank, with a capital of $10,000,000, with authority to issue notes which should be receivable in payment of all dues to the United States, and his recommendations were transferred to the statute book, as they usually were, without material change. The notes were therefore issued and made receivable in payment of public dues. So soon did the good ship of state drift from her moorings into the tempestuous ocean of paper money.

Senator Benton, in 1832, openly asserted on the floor of the Senate that Hamilton purposely overvalued silver, that this metal might furnish the only coins for circulation, thus leading to bank issues as a necessity in the larger exchanges. But it is due to Hamilton to say that he expressed his belief that both metals would circulate, if coined at a ratio of 1 to 15.

CHAPTER IX.

WILD-CAT CURRENCY.

The several States, being prohibited by the Constitution from emitting bills of credit, soon devised a scheme by which money might be made "cheap," and everybody have some of it. New England took the initiative.

Massachusetts, in 1784, had granted a charter to a bank, with power to issue bills without restraint. Soon after the adoption of the Constitution other banks sprang into existence in that section, and, either under the authority of their charters, or in disregard of them, flooded the country with bills which came to be as worthless as those of the Continental Congress. Silver disappearing from circulation, bills as low in denomination as twenty-five cents were issued, on account of the scarcity of coin for change.

Rhode Island, whose colonial history was redolent of bounties, export duties, and industrial loans, outdid her own record in **explosive financial contrivances.**

In 1784 the Farmers' Exchange Bank of Gloucester, in that State, was incorporated, the capital stock to consist of 2,000 shares of $50 each, payable in seven instalments in gold or silver. Some of the stockholders paid in a part for their shares, and gave their notes for the remainder. The directors paid in no money whatever, giving their individual notes for the stock; and the bank commenced operations with only 661 shares issued, on which there had been received any specie, and the total amount of specie received was $11,806.61, most of which was at once drawn out on loans made to the directors. The bank continued to do business for four years, when the stockholders transferred to one Andrew Dexter, Jr., of Boston, a majority of the stock, he borrowing from the bank, on his personal note, the amount necessary to pay for it. This loan he never repaid.

Dexter now having control of the bank, issued at divers times in the course of the year its bills in the amount of $760,285. The only restraint he suffered in the issue of the bills was the physical inability of the cashier to sign them; but to facilitate the issue, this officer went into the country, where he would be undisturbed, and spent his entire time in signing his name to the bills.

For the enormous sum issued, Dexter gave his receipt to the bank, stating that as agent for the bank he would invest it advantageously. Subsequently he took up his receipt, and gave his note for the whole amount, in form as follows: "I, Andrew Dexter, Jr., do promise the President, Directors, and Company of the Farmers' Exchange Bank, to pay them, or order, $-——, in two years from date, with interest at two per cent per annum; it being, however, understood that said Dexter shall not be called upon to make payment until he thinks proper, he being the principal stockholder, and best knowing when it will be proper to pay the same." It is unnecessary to add that he has not yet thought proper to pay the amount.

In 1809 the crash came. Such was the confusion in the accounts of the bank, that the precise amount of bills outstanding could not be ascertained; but the committee appointed by the legislature to investigate its affairs estimated the amount to be $580,000. The specie on hand at that time amounted to $86.46.

In the same year other banks in New England went to the wall, revealing that they had been engaged in transactions as disreputable as those of the Gloucester bank. One bank in Massachusetts was found to have in its vaults only $40 in specie; and another not any. One bank in New Hampshire was in nearly the same situation, with several thousands of bills outstanding. Widespread disaster followed.

The legislature of Massachusetts, to avoid like evils in the future in that State, on January 1, 1810, fixed a penalty of two per cent a month, payable by the bank to bill-holders, for failure or refusal thereafter on its part to redeem its bills on presentation. This proved a salutary restriction.

South of New York, banks were fewer, and there was less disturbance. The issues of the National Bank appeared to have been well sustained, and they kept in check undue issues by other and weaker banks. Its charter expired, however, in 1811; and though the affairs of the bank appeared to have been judiciously managed, Congress refused to renew its charter. The power the bank had exercised in restraining the issues of smaller banks had made it unpopular in many localities, and the advisability of maintaining an institution of such character had become an irritating question in national politics. The same influences which defeated its charter before Congress operated successfully in the State legislature, to which it had made application for a new charter, and the bank was therefore obliged to wind up its affairs.

The field being now cleared, symptoms of mania for bank issues began to develop in the Middle and Western States. In 1814 the legislature of Pennsylvania granted forty-one charters for banks (over the veto of the governor), with an aggregate capital of $17,000,000, of which only one fifth part was required to be paid in. Of the number authorized thirty-seven went into operation, the stockholders in many instances giving their notes for the amount due on their shares. These banks had but a fitful and ephemeral existence, fifteen of them expiring within four years of their organization, hopelessly insolvent.

In 1814 all the banks of the country outside of New England suspended paying specie for their bills. No particular cause can be assigned for the suspension, except the war, and as the war was unpopular in New England the people of that section would accept no excuse of that kind.

In the Middle and Western States a rapid depreciation in the volume of currency took place, and the periodicals of that time are loud in complaints of high prices in those sections, and the greed of the blue-light federalists of New England, which had drawn from them all their specie.

With the return of peace came additional issues of depreciated bank paper, and the abundance of money seemed very gratifying to a great mass of the people. Never before had there been in the country such an appearance of prosperity. The unequal value of the notes in the different localities seemed the only embarrassment; but wealth was accumulating so rapidly that this annoyance was not considered serious, and it was thought that, once accustomed to it, the difficulties would vanish.

In 1815, valuable cargoes of imported goods arrived in Philadelphia, and were eagerly sought for and rapidly sold. Carey called it the "golden age" of Philadelphia, and sneered at the opinion of the superficial reasoner who thought the banks were overtrading.

About this time the mania for paper money had extended to the western frontier. The State of Kentucky incorporated forty new banks, with an aggregate capital of $10,000,000, and no provision for the payment of their notes, of which an enormous amount was issued. Most of these banks failed within a year; still by many writers the period was regarded as the golden age of the West.

In August, 1818, twenty thousand persons in Philadelphia were begging employment, and the question on Market Street was, not who had broken the day before, but who yet stood. In Baltimore and other cities the distress was still greater. Business was virtually at a standstill, and property unsalable at any price. The papers of the day were filled with notices of sheriffs' sales. After all, the golden age had proved a paper one, and not even gilt-edged at that. The evils resulting might have been postponed, but they could not long have been avoided; and the postponement of the evil day would probably have intensified rather than diminished the resulting distress.

Meanwhile the over-issues of the bills of the bank had driven all the coin into New England, where, being in excess of the amount needed for circulation, it had been shipped out of the country, leaving the south and west almost wholly destitute of a circulating medium; and trade by barter was resorted to for want of a better medium. In those days of slow-sailing ships, and of stage-coaches, a readjustment of such a financial disturbance could not at best have been quickly accomplished. Such was the demand for money that a barrel of flour would be given for one dollar of specie, and in Kentucky a gallon of whiskey was willingly exchanged for fifteen cents. The courts refused to grant relief on contracts calling for dollars, and the obligors were consequently ruined.

About this time specie resumption is said to have taken place. But a large majority of the banks issuing notes were out of existence, and if those remaining can be said to have redeemed their notes in coin, it would seem that there are as many degrees of redeemability in a bank as of conscientiousness in man.

The Bank of Darien, Georgia, among others, asserted that it had resumed specie payments, but any person making demands on it for payment of its notes was required, in the presence of the cashier and at least five directors, to make an oath that each and every bill presented was his own, and that he was not an agent for any other person; and to pay on the spot, $1.37½ in specie as a fee on every bill presented, and unless he could find the cashier and five directors together he could not make the oath at all. The newspapers quoted the bills of this period at a discount ranging from five to twenty-five per cent, except in the immediate location of the bank issuing them. Yet all the banks were said to have resumed specie payment.

The rapid rise in the value of the rich lands in the valleys of the Ohio and Mississippi, which were being rapidly settled, furnished such margins of profit that the evils of the depreciated and ever-changing currency could be endured. While in the east some restraint in the issue of bank bills was maintained, in the west and south there was an issue of these bills, known as "wild-cat currency." Many of the banks issuing them had but a nominal capital, consisting mainly of notes given by the stockholders in payment of their shares. In other cases charters of banks authorized by the New England and Southern States were disposed of to non-residents, who organized banks of little or no capital, and the citizens of remote cities suffered great loss from the utter worthlessness of the issues. The various ebbs and floods of currency which alternately stimulated and depressed business until 1836 need not be recounted here. The country prospered, however, despite the monetary evils.

In 1836 the President ordered that only specie should be received in payment for land. This checked the delirium somewhat. Congress, in the following session, passed a bill annulling the provisions of this specie order. The President, however, did not sign it, and as he received it only two days before the close of the session, it failed to become a law. This specie order remained in force until 1862, and was fruitful of naught but good results.

The expansion of the bank issues and loans of 1836 and of the few preceding years could have but one result, and in 1837 the crash came. The State banks suspended, many of them hopelessly involved. The explosion was inevitable, and came none too soon. Several Boston banks even became insolvent, and the Massachusetts country banks were but little better, their issues amounting in some cases to twenty-five to one of specie. The New York banks put forth vigorous efforts to resume, and were generally seconded in their efforts by the banks of the Western and Middle States; and by the end of 1838 resumption was effected by most of the banks in the country, and business was again in its natural channels.

After the reaction of 1839, the country passed

through two years of calm existence. Trade languished, prices were low, and few enterprises proved remunerative; yet the balance of trade with foreign nations was largely in its favor, and the importation of specie had largely increased. The country was not dead, but only taking a needed rest to recuperate its energies after a monetary debauch of half a century. Congress, however, could not let the patient alone, but gave it a tonic in the shape of a protective tariff. The patient recovered, and the political doctors have not failed, in all the subsequent advertisements of their nostrum, to mention the wonderful cure.

During the fourteen years following, the country passed through alternate periods of gloom and hope. The war with Mexico brought about a financial "squeeze," but caused no special monetary disturbance. Again immigration began to flow largely into the Western States, and new enterprises were pushed much beyond the need of the settlers. In the summer of 1857 the Ohio Life and Trust Company, the credit of which had been very high, failed for several millions of liabilities. This failure gave a shock to the exchange in New York, and stocks fell off from thirty to fifty per cent. The banks were caught with a large amount of issues and loans outstanding, against a very small reserve of specie. The banks of the New England States held a reserve against deposits and issues of only about eight per cent; and the banks throughout the country held on an average only about sixteen per cent. With so small a reserve there can be no surprise that the banks were unable to meet at once the demands which were made upon them, although in the end most of them proved to be solvent.

The State of New York had especially guarded against the suspension of specie payments by its banks. The issues of their notes were required to be secured by deposits of State stocks in the hands of a government officer, and the constitution of the State itself provided that no law should be passed authorizing the banks, under any circumstances, to suspend specie payments. Yet the banks did suspend, and the judges of the court agreed not to issue any injunctions to prevent such action, unless there was some evidence that the banks were acting fraudulently.

The panic which ensued created considerable distress in the money centres, but the country was generally prosperous, and early in the next year the banks throughout the country had resumed payments of their bills in specie, not to suspend again until the great events of the coming civil war pressed heavily upon them. With the civil war came a radical change in the monetary system of the country.

CHAPTER X.

THE TREASURY CORNERED.

In 1814 the country was at war with Great Britain. Anticipating the revenues for 1813, Congress, the preceding year, authorized the issue of interest-bearing Treasury notes, which should be received in payment of all dues to the government, the interest to be computed at $1\frac{1}{2}$ cents per day on $100. The notes were not a legal tender, but might be paid to any one willing to take them. These were the first notes intended to circulate as money which were issued under the present Constitution. Fifty millions were issued. The advocates of their issue claimed that the scheme was only a method of discounting the revenue, and so, in fact, was only another form for a loan; but the notes had a considerable circulation as money.

The government, hesitating to levy a tax, borrowed what it could from the banks outside of New England. The revenues were further anticipated by additional issues of Treasury notes, all of which bore interest except that portion of the loan issued in 1815 of less denomination than $100. These small notes were evidently designed to supplant the depreciated bank-notes in circulation. No one was compelled to take them, but they circulated as money, and were, like the interest-bearing notes, receivable in payment of dues to the government.

The whole country was now embarrassed by the different values of the currency afloat. The Treasury Department was perplexed in conducting the fiscal affairs of the government. It was compelled to accept payment of duties and taxes in the legal currency of the place of payment. It attempted to accept only notes which were accepted at par in the locality where received, but the depository banks in which the accounts were kept took advantage of this restriction and credited the Treasury with only their own notes, at par. They received, however, the notes of other banks, but held them as special deposits, constituting a discredited fund upon which the Treasury drew, only to provoke the wrath of the payee of the check, to whom the government owed a just debt. With every bank the Treasury was obliged to keep four accounts, to wit: —

1st. An account of cash, meaning, in the absence of coin, legal currency.

2d. An account of special deposits of bank-notes, being notes issued by banks other than the depository.

3d. An account of special deposit of Treasury notes bearing interest.

4th. An account of deposits of small Treasury notes not bearing interest.

The Secretary of the Treasury naïvely remarked that, in selecting the funds from which the government obligations were to be paid, he considered the character of the debt, and the person to whom payment was to be made.

In such a condition of affairs, Mr. Dallas, Secretary of the Treasury, recommended to Congress the re-establishment of a national bank, with a capital of $50,000,000, of which the government should subscribe $20,000,000, in six per cent stock; the remainder to be subscribed by individuals, $6,000,000 to be paid in specie, $6,000,000 in Treasury notes, and $18,000,000 in six per cent stock. The bank was to be bound to loan $30,000,000 to the government, and was authorized to suspend specie payments whenever the President of the United States should deem such suspension advisable. Its establishment was urged mainly upon the ground that its notes, even if depreciated, would furnish a uniform currency, in which exchanges might be paid, and the fiscal operations of the government conducted.

A bill embodying the recommendations of the

Secretary was introduced in Congress, but the House struck out the clause authorizing the bank to suspend specie payments, and modified several other provisions of the bill. After considerable delay and compromising between the two houses, the bill passed; but the President vetoed it, giving, as one reason, that the bank would be unable to maintain specie payments. Fortunately the war ended, and no further action was taken in the matter.

The Treasury balance, though in amount much in excess of any apparent necessity, consisted mainly of unavailable bank-notes, and to meet the payment of interest falling due a loan had to be issued. The Secretary, in his annual report for 1815, thus portrays his troubles:—

"At the close of the last session of Congress, the demands on the Treasury were interesting in their nature, as well as great in their amount. . . . The efficiency of the means which were possessed for the liquidation of these demands depended upon circumstances beyond the control of the government. The balance of money in the Treasury consisted of bank credits, lying chiefly in the southern and western sections of the Union.

"The suspension of specie payments throughout the greater portion of the United States, and the consequent cessation of the interchange of bank-notes and bank credits between the institutions of the different States, had deprived the Treasury of all the facilities of transferring its funds from place to place; and a proposition which was made, at an early period, to the principal banks of the commercial cities on the line of the Atlantic, with a view in some degree to restore those facilities, could not be effected for the want of a concurrence in the requisite number of banks. Hence it has happened (and the duration of the evil is without any positive limitation) that, however adequate the public revenue may be, in its general product, to discharge the public engagements, it becomes totally inadequate in the process of its application, since the possession of public funds in one part no longer affords the evidence of a fiscal capacity to discharge a public debt in any other part of the Union.

"From the suspension of specie payments, and from various other causes, real or imaginary, differences in the rate of exchange arose between the several States, and even between the several districts in the same State; and the embarrassments of the Treasury were more and more increased, since Congress had not sanctioned any allowance on account of the rate of exchange, and the amount of the legislative appropriations was the same wherever the legislative objects were to be effected. But the Treasury notes partook of the inequalities of the exchange in the transactions of individuals, although the Treasury could only issue them at their par value. The public stock, created in consideration of a loan, also partook of the inequalities of the exchange, although, to the government, the value of the stock created, and the obligation of the debt to be discharged were the same, wherever the subscription to the loan might be made.

"Thus, notwithstanding the ample revenue provided and permanently pledged for the payment of the public creditor, and notwithstanding the auspicious influence of peace upon the resources of the nation, the market price of the Treasury notes and of the public stock was everywhere far below its par or true value for a considerable period after the adjournment of Congress, vibrating, however, with a change of place, from the rate of seventy-five to the rate of ninety per cent. Payments in bank paper were universally preferred, during that period, to payments in the paper of the government; and it was a natural consequence that, wherever the Treasury failed in procuring a local currency, it failed also in making a stipulated payment.

"Under these extraordinary and perplexing circumstances the great effort of the Treasury was, 1st, to provide promptly and effectually for all urgent demands, at the proper place of payment, and for the requisite amount of funds; 2d, to overcome the difficulties of the circulating medium, so far as it was practicable, so that no creditor should receive more, and no debtor pay less, in effective value, on the same account, than every other creditor or every other debtor; and, 3d, to avoid any unreasonable sacrifice of the public property, particularly when it must also be attended with a sacrifice of the public credit. It was not expected that this effort would everywhere produce the same satisfaction and the same results; but the belief is entertained that it has been successful in the attainment of its objects, to the extent of a just anticipation."

CHAPTER XI.

THE SECOND UNITED STATES BANK.

Congress on the 10th of April, 1816, authorized a United States Bank at Philadelphia. The charter was limited to twenty years, and the capital fixed at $35,000,000, $7,000,000 of which was to be subscribed by the government, payable in coin or in United States stocks; the remainder by individuals, one-fourth payable in coin, and three-fourths in coin or United States stock. Branches of this bank were authorized at several places, and the notes of the bank payable on demand were made receivable in all payments to the United States. The moneys of the government were to be deposited in the bank or its branches, and the penalty imposed upon the bank for refusing to pay its notes or deposits in coin, on demand, was fixed at twelve per cent per annum, until the amount due was paid. In consideration of the privileges conferred by Congress, the bank was to pay to the United States $1,500,000. It went into operation in January, 1817, at perhaps the worst stage of the monetary troubles of that period. From the outset it was surrounded by difficulties.

In April, 1818, the amount of its discounts and exchange balance had swollen to $43,000,000, but it had been able to put into circulation less than the amount of $10,000,000; not on account of any disinclination of parties to receive the notes, but because the president and cashier could not sign as many as were wanted. Application was therefore made to Congress for authority for like officers in the branch banks to sign notes, but Congress refused, alleging that such action would prevent that uniformity of notes for which the bank had been specially created. The bank, to sustain itself, imported specie in exchange for the funded debt it held, but, there being no demand for it for circulation, it was exported by individuals as rapidly as imported by the bank, and at no time was there an amount of over $3,000,000 in its vaults.

In July, 1818, the bank began to curtail its discounts and demand payment of all obligations due from other banks, alleging that such action was necessary on account of the premium on specie. In three months and ten days a reduction in discount was made amounting to $4,500,000, mainly in the four principal cities. This sudden contraction had a disastrous effect upon the merchants, and through them upon the rest of the community. The bank also ordered that the mother bank at Philadelphia should thereafter receive no notes except its own; and each one of the branches no notes except those of that one branch. The mother bank called upon the branch banks for the payment of their respective obligations, and they in turn had to call in their own loans sharply, bringing great distress and many failures in business.

About this time whisperings were heard that Congress was coming to the relief of the country in some mysterious way. Niles, in his Register of October 3, intimated that a grand scheme was on foot to keep the paper-mill going — nothing less than the substitution of a paper currency as a legal tender instead of coin. In his Register of November 7 he says, —

"We have several times darkly hinted at a great intrigue which was going on to relieve the banking system, generally, and especially to subserve the grand views of the Bank of the United States. I am just now informed of what this intrigue is; but private honor will not permit me to mention it at present. The object is, by bits of paper to prevent the banks from being compelled to pay their debts. This is the long and short of the whole affair. Aye, and the pretence is most specious, the appearance most seducing, but the instantaneous effect will be to banish money, and bring about those happy times when lordly banks issued notes for six and a quarter cents, and a copper coin was a rarity. . . . Upon my conscience I would rather agree to have a hereditary President and a Senate for life than that this thing should happen. In the latter case our President and Senators might be influenced to good actions by a sense of individual shame or a love of true glory, and the choice of representatives would be left free to us; but in the other, an unknown and irresistible aristocracy would be raised up, secret as the Council of Ten and remorseless as the Holy Inquisition. Give me to live under any despotism but that which springs from the command of money; for it is the most base and unprincipled of all.

"But Congress will not, cannot, dare not, pass the law proposed to pamper speculation. They may prohibit the exportation of coin if they please; still they cannot substitute a paper medium for it, and compel me to take it in payment of debts justly due me. And this it is which is fondly designed to be attempted — for the benefit of the rag-barons."

No relief came, however, and on the 9th of April, 1819, at a meeting of the directors of the bank, means of relief were agreed to as follows: " To continue the curtailment of discount, to forbid the branch offices south and west to issue their notes when exchanges were against them; to collect balances due by local banks to the offices; to ask of the government time to transfer moneys from one office to another, as they might be needed for disbursement, and to obtain a loan in Europe for $2,500,000." These measures were actively carried into effect, and they lifted the bank from extreme prostration to a state of safety and some power, but at the expense of the local banks and the business community. "The bank saved itself, but the people were ruined," says one writer.

In 1832 the bank applied to Congress for a renewal of its charter, which would expire in 1836. Congress passed a bill for its re-charter, but it was vetoed by the President July 10, 1832. The bank had specie enough to pay all its obligations to the government, but it kept up the stringency for political effect, and used its power and influence to embarrass and defeat the administration. Probably the affairs of the bank had not at all times been administered with wisdom and discretion; but in 1830 the finance committee of the Senate had said: "They are satisfied that the country is in the enjoyment of a uniform national currency, not only sound and uniform in itself, but perfectly adapted to the purposes of the government and the community, and more sound and uniform than that possessed by any other nation."

On the 23d of September, 1833, announcement was made that on the first of the next month the public deposits would be removed to the State banks. The transfer was made, and it created a political turmoil of unprecedented bitterness. The State banks receiving the public deposits, being favored by large importations of specie, expanded their loans and circulation, and another wave of speculation rolled over the country. Money being plenty, and dividends easily obtained, immense purchases of public land was made by speculators, for which the government was paid largely in notes of State banks, of questionable values. With the largely increased receipts the government paid off its entire indebtedness, and still had nearly fifty millions, for which it had no use, lying idle in the banks. This idle capital stimulated the fever of speculation already fiercely raging.

The bank did not wind up its affairs in anticipation of the expiration of its charter in 1836, but obtained another charter from the legislature of Pennsylvania. The act granting it was entitled "An act to repeal the State taxes on real and personal property, and to continue and extend the improvement of the State by railroads and canals; and to charter a State bank to be called a United States bank." The obligations imposed upon the bank in consideration of the issue of this charter could not have fallen short of $5,000,000, if it had lived long enough to meet the charges imposed. The bank suspended specie payments with the State banks, and soon after organizing under its new charter succumbed to trials which perhaps more prudent management might have averted.

A financial giant, however, such as was this institution, did not expire without a struggle. In 1839 it got the New York banks in its toils, and brought them to the verge of ruin. Two years later, Sampson-like, it laid hold of the pillars of the financial temple, and signalized its death by a general crash. The circulating notes and deposits of this soulless corporation were eventually paid in full, but no dividends were paid to the stockholders. The whole $28,000,000 subscribed was a loss to them. The government, in the end, lost nothing by the bank; but the action of the President in severing from it all fiscal operations of the government appears at this day to have been justifiable and fortunate.

CHAPTER XII.

UNITED STATES NOTES.

FROM 1857 to 1861 the country enjoyed abundant prosperity. The value of its exports to foreign countries during these three years exceeded that of its imports by $100,000,000. The banks held a strong reserve of specie, and their circulation was not deemed excessive. In 1860 their circulation was $207,000,000 and their deposits $254,000,000, against which amounts was held a reserve of $103,000,000, of which $80,000,000 was specie.

Notwithstanding the general prosperity of the country, the public expenditures had since 1857 been greater than the receipts to the amount of about $90,000,000, which deficit had been provided for by public loans.

Congress met in December, 1860. The government was threatened with disruption by civil war. The public offices at Washington were filled mainly by the conspirators themselves, or those in sympathy with them. The public treasury was empty, and the public credit impaired.

How to meet the current expenses of the government was the problem which confronted this Congress.

Measures for issuing another loan were immediately taken, and on December 17 an act was approved authorizing the issue of $10,000,000 of Treasury notes, payable in one year, to bear the lowest rate of interest at which the notes could be sold at par. The rates ranged from six to twelve per cent per annum. In the month of February, following, the necessities of the government compelled the issuing of another loan. This was not to exceed $25,000,000, was to run twenty years, and bear interest at six per cent. About $18,000,000 were issued at the rate of $100 of loan for $89.03 in specie.

On March 22, 1861 another loan was authorized — this time Treasury notes to bear six per cent interest, and to run two years. They were made receivable in all payments to the government, and consequently were disposed of at a slight premium.

Before the issue of these notes was authorized many of the Southern members had left Congress to participate in the Rebellion. Two days after the approval of the act Mr. Lincoln was inaugurated as President, and a few days later Mr. Salmon P. Chase was confirmed as Secretary of the Treasury.

On July 4 Congress convened by special proclamation of the President. Eleven States were in actual rebellion. Seventy-five thousand volunteers had been called into the field, and the capital city was a military camp. The Secretary of the Treasury called upon Congress for means to meet the extraordinary expenses. He estimated the expenditures for the year ending June 30, 1862, at $318,000,000. Vast and unprecedented as was this sum, it proved $240,000,000 less than the amount expended.

Congress, in answer to the call, on July 17 authorized a loan of $200,000,000, and provided that $50,000,000 thereof might be in Treasury notes in denominations of not less than $5, payable on demand, not bearing interest, and reissuable until December 31, 1862. They were known as demand notes.

The first instalment of these notes was issued in August following, and was paid to the clerks in the departments for salaries, and to other creditors of the government. Although redeemable at sight in coin, the notes were received with reluctance; and to give them credit the principal officers of the Treasury Department signed a paper agreeing to accept them in payment of their salaries. Many of the banks refused to take them at par, but as the government accepted them in payment of dues they soon came to be preferred to the notes of the State banks.

At this time the banks had increased their specie reserve to $87,000,000, their circulation and deposits remaining substantially unchanged.

To the banks the Secretary applied for an advance of $50,000,000, in the form of a loan for seven-thirty three-year bonds; the amount to be reimbursed to the banks, as far as practicable, from the proceeds of similar bonds to be sold throughout the country direct to the people, through loan agencies which had been established.

On August 19 representatives of the leading banks in New York, Boston, and Philadelphia met the Secretary in the first named city, and a full and unreserved conference was held. The banks demanded better terms than the Secretary offered, but this official was firm, and expressed a hope that they would take the loan on the terms he offered. "If not," he said, "I will go back to Washington and issue notes for circulation, for it is certain the war must go on until the rebellion is put down, if we have to put out paper until it takes a thousand dollars to buy a breakfast."

The banks advanced the $50,000,000 needed, in specie, of which about $45,000,000 was returned to them from the proceeds of public subscriptions, and for the remainder seven-thirty three-year bonds were issued as provided; and the alternative presented by Mr. Chase was avoided. The reimbursements to the banks enabled them to make another loan in like manner upon the same terms, and through these means the Secretary obtained at par $100,000,000 in specie for three years at $7\frac{3}{10}$ per cent interest per annum.

This showed a marked improvement in the condition of the public credit. Three months before, when there was a strong probability that the war might be averted, the government paid as high as twelve per cent for a portion of a loan of $10,000,000. But now the government, although smarting from the humiliating wounds of Bull Run, obtained ten times the amount at a rate of interest much more favorable. Confidence in the measures and the men of the new administration, as compared with those of the former one, was the main instrument in bringing about this favorable change. Patriotism, perhaps, went for something.

Abroad, however, especially in England, the credit of the country was at a very low ebb. On Sunday, after the defeat at Bull Run, the British agent at Washington for the London bankers through whom our government business was transacted, called upon Mr. Harrington, Assistant Secretary of the Treasury, to give security for the balance due of about $40,000. Mr. Harrington directed him to call on Monday, as the government would not probably break up before business hours next day.

The London *Times* concluded an article about these operations by exclaiming: "What strength, what resources, what vitality, what energy there must be in a nation that is able to ruin itself on a scale so transcendent and magnificent."

The pressure for providing means for carrying on the war still continued, however, and the Secretary applied to the banks for a third loan. They were unwilling to take any more of the seven-thirty bonds, as little market could be found for them among their customers. The Secretary therefore offered, and the banks accepted, $50,000,000 of the twenty-year loan, authorized by act of July 17, 1861, a sufficient discount being allowed to make the loan equivalent to one bearing interest at seven per cent, a less rate than that of the notes.

Meanwhile the banks had persistently and constantly urged the Secretary to forego the issue of Treasury notes, which were circulating as money, and to draw upon them for coin in payment of their subscriptions.

To a question of the Secretary the New York banks replied: "In New York we are entirely willing to pay in coin; in any other cities in whatever funds the check holders may demand, in coin if the creditors insist upon coin and the bank is willing and able to pay in coin, but otherwise in bank-notes."

To this the Secretary would not consent, although at that time no payment to public creditors in coin, when demanded, had been refused by any of the banks. He said: "If you can lend me all the coin required to conduct the operations of the war, or show me where I can borrow it elsewhere at fair rates, I will withdraw every note already issued, and pledge myself never to issue another; but if you cannot, you must let me stick to United States notes, and increase their issue just so far as the deficiency of coin may make necessary." This was the reply of Secretary Chase on November 16, 1861, to the bankers with whom he had just negotiated the $50,000,000 loan.

The policy therein avowed was the first step taken towards that inflation of the currency which subsequently played so important a part in all the affairs of the country, and from whose unhappy effect we are not yet free.

The necessity of taking such a step is far from evident. The government during that year had negotiated $250,000,000 of loans, of which less than $30,000,000 was in Treasury notes. These notes, however, had come into competition with the paper issues of the banks, and were rapidly driving them from the channels of circulation which they had previously occupied. The bank-notes, not being needed for circulation, were returned to the banks for redemption. As the banks were putting forth their best energies to place the loans they had taken of the government, they naturally did not want their notes to come in at that time for redemption, as they inevitably must if the issue of Treasury notes continued, and the urgent demand of the banks upon the Secretary to put no more Treasury notes in circulation seems natural and proper.

Had the Secretary yielded to the request of the banks, and the government accepted the bank issues in payment of dues, the demand for such issues would have increased rather than diminished; the banks would have been relieved from any necessity of redeeming them in coin, and could easily have paid specie to the government for the loan which they had just taken. But the resolution of the Secretary was unalterable, and the evil which he was trying to prevent became inevitable. The banks being obliged to take care of their notes, and at the same time to pay specie to the government, were unable to meet the demands upon them, or at least thought they were, and on December 27, 1861, they yielded to the pressure and suspended specie payment.

For this action the Secretary appears to be mainly responsible. The amount of outstanding circulation of the banks had at that time been reduced $183,000,000, and the specie reserve increased to $102,000,000; and during the fiscal year of 1861 the excess of imports of specie over exports amounted to more than $16,000,000, a balance more favorable than that of any year since 1847. Careful estimates since made have fixed the amount of specie in circulation at the time of the suspension at about $250,000,000. Of this amount not over $42,000,000 was in fractional silver; the remainder was in gold coin, no silver dollars being in circulation. The large expenditures of the government for 1861 had been made in specie, but this specie, when paid out, soon found its way back to the banks where it was needed, and there had been at no time during the year the slightest embarrassment arising from any lack of specie as a circulating medium. In the action taken by the Secretary there was nothing to be gained, and experience has shown that the integrity of the country was to be lost.

Consequent upon the action of the banks there was but one thing for the government to do, and it did it. On January 1, 1862, it dishonored its own promises — it ceased paying coin. Gold was immediately at a premium, in paper, of two per cent, and the Secretary, who would not in November employ bank notes circulating at par, was compelled to make payments to creditors in the government's own depreciated paper. In fleeing from an imaginary Scylla he had struck a real Charybdis.

Congress, meanwhile, was actively preparing

measures for raising more money. Mr. Spaulding, a member of the House from New York, and chairman of a sub-committee of the Ways and Means Committee, prepared and reported a bill which attracted much attention. For the first time in the history of the country it was seriously proposed to issue bills made a legal tender in payment of debts.

Much opposition to the legal-tender clause was expressed by leading papers throughout the country. Delegates from some of the banks in New York, Boston, and Philadelphia appeared in Washington to oppose the bill. They invited the Finance Committee of the Senate, and the Committee of Ways and Means of the House, to meet them at the office of the Secretary of the Treasury on January 11, 1862. The invitation was accepted, and the convention assembled accordingly at the Treasury Department. The whole scheme was thoroughly discussed, and the New York "Tribune" reported the discussion as follows:

"The sub-committee of Ways and Means, through Mr. Spaulding, objected to any and every form of 'shinning' by government through Wall or State streets to begin with; objected to the knocking down of government stocks to seventy-five or sixty cents on the dollar, the inevitable result of throwing a new and large loan on the market without limitation as to price; claimed for Treasury notes as much virtue of par value as the notes of banks which have suspended specie payment, but which yet circulate in the trade of the north; and finished with firmly refusing to assent to any scheme which should promote a speculation by brokers, bankers, and others in the government securities, and particularly any scheme which should double the public debt of the country, and double the expenses of the war by damaging the credit of the government to the extent of sending it to 'shin' through the shaving shops of New York, Boston, and Philadelphia. He affirmed his conviction, as a banker and legislator, that it was the lawful policy, as well as the manifest duty, of the government in the present exigency to legalize as tender its fifty millions issue of demand Treasury notes, authorized at the extra session in July last, and to add to this stock of legal tender, immediately, one hundred millions more. He thought that this financial measure would carry the country through the war, and save its credit and its dignity; at the same time we should insist upon taxation abundantly ample to pay the expenses of the government on a peace footing, and interest on every dollar of the public obligations, and to give this generation a clear show of a speedy liquidation of the public debt."

It does not appear, however, that the views of the several delegates and those of the public officials were brought into harmony.

On January 22, 1862, a bill was introduced in

the House authorizing the issue of $500,000,000 six per cent bonds, and $100,000,000 of Treasury notes. The framers of the bill had concluded to make the notes authorized a legal tender, and the bill therefore provided that there should be printed on the back of the notes the following words: "The within note is a legal tender in payment of all debts, public and private, and is exchangeable for bonds of the United States bearing six per cent interest."

This legal tender provision was ably and thoroughly discussed in the House. The Secretary urged the passage of the bill, though expressing a strong dislike to making anything but coin a legal tender in payment of debt. He hoped that the notes would be speedily converted into bonds, and the bonds made a basis for the circulation of the banks; and with this hope he became reconciled to the enactment of a measure which as Chief Justice he afterwards declared to be unconstitutional.

The measure was opposed by all the Democratic members of the House, and by many of the prominent Republicans; and even the friends of the measure gave it only a reluctant support, regretting the necessity which seemed to call for a measure fraught with so many possible evils.

A prominent Democratic member urged that the policy of forcing a paper currency upon the country was a dangerous experiment; that it would lead to other issues; that gold and silver would be banished from circulation, and an immense inflation would take place. "Cheap in materials, easy of issue, worked by steam, signed by machinery, there will be no end to the legion of paper devils which shall issue forth from the loins of the Secretary."

In after years, and when his vision proved a reality, he and most of his party friends defended the "paper devils," declaring that the machine-made currency was the best the world ever saw, so good, in fact, that nobody would take it from us. The opinions of such men need not therefore be further considered at present.

Mr. Morrill, of Vermont, at present a senator from that State, opposed with much ability the provisions of the bill making notes a legal tender, declaring that if so made they would, to the extent that they were tendered as public dues, be a forced loan, and that, to the extent of the difference between their current value and that of standard coin, they would be a breach of public faith; that upon their issue the cost of carrying on the war would be vastly increased; that prices would go up; and that the addition we should pile upon our national debt would prove that it might have been wiser to have burned our paper dollars before they were issued.

Mr. Roscoe Conkling, of New York, opposed

the measure with his characteristic vehemence. He declared that the country was full of wealth; that the harvests had been abundant; that nearly every loyal State teemed with the elements of material prosperity; that the passage of the act would proclaim throughout the country a saturnalia of fraud, a carnival for rogues; that every person who had received for others money would release himself from liability by paying back in the spurious money which we should put afloat; that everybody would do it except those who are more honest than the American Congress advised them to be. He declared that the whole scheme presupposed that the notes to be emitted would be lepers in the commercial world from the hour they were brought into it; that they would be shunned and condemned by the laws of trade and value. If that was not to be their fate, there was no sense in attempting to legislate upon their value. He believed that all the money needed could be provided in season by means of unquestionable legality and safety.

Mr. Lovejoy, of Illinois, also opposed the bill. He did not believe it was in the power of any legislative body to make something out of nothing; that a piece of paper stamped as five dollars, unless it was convertible at sight into a five-dollar gold piece, was not five dollars, but a delusion and a fallacy.

He proposed the following, which would seem to have been a vigorous outline of the policy which would be commended by the opponents of the bill:

"1st. Adequate taxation, if need be, to the extent of $200,000,000.

"2d. Adopt legislation that shall compel all banking institutions to do a business on a specie basis. Every piece of paper that claimed to be money, but was not, I would chase back to the man or corporation that forged it, and visit upon them the penalties of the law. I would not allow a bank-note to circulate that was not constantly, conveniently, and certainly convertible into specie.

"3d. I would issue interest-bearing bonds of the United States, and go into market and borrow money and pay the obligations of the government. This would be honest, business-like, and, in the end, economical. This could be done. Other channels of investment are blocked up, and capital would seek the bonds for investment."

And he added: "This is, in substance, what I propose. This would bring us through the war poor indeed, for half the nation has to support the other half, but with the health and vigor of the athlete, and not with the bloated flesh of the beer guzzler. Did I not know that the passage of this bill was a foregone conclusion, I would move to recommit, with instructions to that effect."

Mr. Spaulding, the putative father of the bill,

summed up his ideas by stating, in effect, that if the notes were given a legal-tender quality they would become a standard of value, and, compared with themselves, they would not depreciate. The statement suggests Mr. Bunsby.

Mr. Stevens, chairman of the Ways and Means Committee, closed the debate, speaking urgently in favor of the bill. He argued at length upon the constitutionality of the measure, taking the ground that Congress alone could decide whether the measure was necessary and proper to raise and support armies, this discretion having been confided to it by the Constitution; and once decided by that department no other department of the government could re-judge it. The Supreme Court might think the judgment of Congress erroneous, but they could not review it. Concluding that the measure was constitutional, he inquired as to its expediency.

"All admit the necessity of the issue, but some object to their being made money. It is not easy to see how notes issued without being made immediately payable in specie can be made any worse by making them a legal tender, and yet that is the whole argument so far as expediency is concerned. Other gentlemen argue this would impair contracts by making the debt payable in other money than that which existed at the time of the contract, and would so be unconstitutional. Where do gentlemen find any prohibition on Congress against passing laws impairing contracts? There is none, though it would be unjust to do it; but this impairs no contract. All contracts are made not only with a view to present laws, but subject to the future legislation of the country."

Later he stated: " Our project proposes United States notes secured at the end of twenty years, to be paid in coin, and the interest raised by taxation semi-annually; such notes to be money, and of uniform value throughout the Union."

From this it would appear that the policy of paying the bonds at maturity in depreciated notes, as afterwards advocated by him, was an afterthought on his part.

The bill passed the House by a vote of ninety-three to fifty-nine. It increased the amount of the proposed issue to $150,000,000, of which $50,000,000 were to be issued in lieu of the same amount of notes authorized by act of July 17, 1861.

The bill was immediately sent to the Senate, and there referred to the committee on finance, of which Mr. Fessenden was chairman.

Meanwhile the Secretary, fearing that the Treasury might be embarrassed by the probable delay in procuring the passage of the bill, asked authority to issue $10,000,000 of Treasury notes in addition to the $50,000,000 already authorized.

A bill to that effect was promptly passed, and became a law February 12, 1862.

Mr. Fessenden reported the House bill to the Senate with certain amendments, of which the most important ones were:

That the notes should be receivable in all claims against the United States, of whatever kind, except for interest on bonds and notes, which should be paid in coin; and another section was added providing that all duties on imported goods and proceeds of the sale of lands should be set apart to pay coin interest on the debt, and, of the remainder, a certain portion for a sinking-fund.

The bill did not yet provide that the duties on imports should be paid in coin.

Mr. Fessenden opposed the bill in a lengthy speech.

He saw no reason for a loss of credit by the conduct of the war. He alleged that a measure of this kind could not increase confidence in the ability or integrity of the country; that it was, in fact, a confession of bankruptcy; that we began with a declaration that we were unable to pay or to borrow, and that such a declaration was not calculated to increase our credit; that it would inflict a stain upon the national honor; that it would change the value of all property; that there would follow inflation, subsequent depression, and all the evils which flow from an inflated currency;

and that the loss would fall most heavily upon the poor by reason of the inflation.

Mr. Collamer, of Vermont, claimed that the bill was unconstitutional, and even if it was a necessity he could not vote for it; that there were two modes of replenishing the Treasury, one by taxation, and the other by borrowing money; that to borrow money there must be a lender and a borrower, and both should act voluntarily, and that the borrower should not compel the lender to part with his money without an inducement; and that the operation of the bill was not as honorable or honest as a forced loan. He had no doubt the country was able to sustain itself pecuniarily as well as physically. He, for one, desired that it should; he did not want it done by saying that now, because the necessity requires money, he would go and steal it or authorize anybody else to steal it.

Mr. Sherman made an elaborate speech in favor of the bill, grounding his argument upon the necessities of the hour.

He stated that $100,000,000 was then due the army, and that $250,000,000 more would be due by July 1; that the banks had already exhausted their capital in making loans to the government; that bonds could not be sold except at great sacrifice, because there was no money to buy them; that bonds could not be sold for gold and silver, which was then the only money which could be received under the sub-treasury law, and that it was necessary to make the currency a legal tender to aid in making further loans. The only objection he had to the measure was, that too many notes might be issued. He did not believe the issue of $150,000,000 would do any harm; it was only a temporary expedient, however, and should not be repeated.

Mr. Sumner also favored the bill in an elaborate and able speech. He recognized that in the exigency money must be had; and he argued that the Constitution gave ample powers to Congress to clothe the notes proposed to be issued with legal tender power. Still he thought it was hard, very hard, to think that a country so powerful, so rich, and so beloved should be compelled to adopt a policy of even questionable propriety. He argued that we must of necessity maintain the integrity of the government, and must all set our faces against any proposition like the present, except as a temporary expedient rendered imperative by the exigencies of the hour. "Others may doubt if the exigency is sufficiently imperative; but the Secretary of the Treasury, whose duty it is to understand the occasion, does not doubt. In his opinion the war requires the sacrifice. Uncontrollable passions have been let loose to overturn tranquil conditions of peace. Meanwhile your soldiers in the field must be paid and fed. Here, then, can be no failure or postponement. A remedy which at another moment you would reject is now proposed. Whatever may be the national resources, they are not now within reach, except by summary process. Reluctantly, painfully, I consent that the process should issue. And yet I cannot give such a vote without warning the government against the dangers from such an experiment. The medicine of the Constitution must not become its daily bread. Nor can I disguise the conviction that better than any legal tender will be vigorous, earnest efforts for the suppression of the rebellion, and for the establishment of the Constitution in its true principles over the territory which the rebellion has usurped."

Mr. Doolittle moved to limit the legal tender clause to "debts thereafter contracted;" but the amendment was not adopted.

The bill passed the Senate by a vote of thirty to seven, Mr. Fessenden finally waiving his scruples and voting for it.

In the House the Senate amendments met with determined opposition. It was alleged that they created two kinds of money, one for the bondholder, and one for the other creditors of the country; that in providing coin to be paid for interest the government had tied its hands, as nobody could tell where the coin was to come from.

Mr. Stevens especially opposed the amendments, declaring that we were discriminating against the notes and thus depreciating their value at the outset. He said it was his expectation that no more of the notes would ever be issued, and that by using them for all purposes as money they could be easily maintained at par with coin; and he hoped and expected they would be.

Most of the Senate amendments were, however, concurred in. A final conference between the two houses added a clause providing, that duties on imported goods should be paid in coin.

The bill became a law on the February 25, 1862. It authorized the issue of $150,000,000 United States notes, not bearing interest, payable to bearer, of such denominations as the Secretary of the Treasury might deem expedient, not less than five dollars each; that $50,000,000 of this issue should be used in taking up the notes issued under the act of July 17, 1861; that the notes should be receivable in payment of all taxes, internal duties, excises, debts, and demands of every kind due to the United States except duties on imports, and all claims and demands against the United States of every kind whatsoever, except, however, interest upon bonds and notes, which should be paid in coin; and that the notes should also be lawful money and legal tender in payment of all debts public and private within the United

States, except duties on imports and interest as before stated. It also provided that the notes might be converted into the six per cent bonds authorized by the act, and that the notes might be reissued from time to time as the exigencies of the public service should require.

It is noticeable that throughout all the debate only reluctant support was given to the measure; that its friends believed that the evils apprehended would be counteracted by the authority to convert the notes into interest-bearing bonds; and that the notes themselves, taking the place of the issues of the State banks, would furnish a circulating medium, the demand for which would be such as to keep them substantially at par with specie

CHAPTER XIII.

ADDITIONAL ISSUES.

The act authorizing the issue of United States notes contained no pledge against additional issues, but it was generally understood that no more of the notes were to be put into circulation. But $150,000,000 was not enough, and, upon the recommendation of Secretary Chase, Congress passed a bill, which the President approved March 17, 1862, making the $60,000,000 of outstanding demand notes a legal tender for the same purpose and to a like extent as the United States notes, the reason being that, as the demand notes were payable on demand in coin, they ought to circulate at par, but being slightly depreciated, some of the banks had refused to accept them as money from their customers. With a legal tender quality, these notes, it was thought, would pass "without loss to the holders." These were the notes which the Secretary, in the previous November, had insisted upon putting in circulation, that public creditors might not, in a possible contingency, be required to accept bank-notes, although bank-notes, at that time, were circulating at par with gold.

The newly authorized notes were speedily put into circulation, and were received throughout the country with great favor. When the entire amount authorized had been put into circulation, gold was quoted at only $104\frac{1}{2}$, and the friends of the scheme congratulated each other that they had done no worse. The expenses of the war were, however, largely exceeding expectations, and on June 17, 1862, Secretary Chase applied to Congress for authority to issue $150,000,000 more of such notes, of which sum $35,000,000 was to be in denominations of less than five dollars. He asserted that, in making payments to the army, great inconvenience had been occasioned in satisfying demands of less than that amount; that where coin reached the creditor, it was not held, but passed immediately to sutlers and others, and disappeared from circulation, a result which would have required no prophet to foresee. He added, "It may properly be further observed, that since the United States notes are made a legal tender, and maintained nearly at the par of gold, by the provision for their conversion into bonds bearing six per cent interest, payable in coin, it is not easy to see why small notes may not be issued as widely as large ones." He further stated that the daily receipts from customs were about $230,000, and that the daily conversion of the United States notes into bonds did not exceed $150,000, while the daily expenditures could not be estimated at less than $1,000,000, and that he had already exhausted the issue of the notes authorized by the act of February 25, 1862.

The application of the Secretary was promptly granted. Congress now seemed willing to increase the supply of notes, if, by that method of raising money, recourse to taxation, a plan always unpopular, could be avoided. And so the additional issue asked for was authorized July 11, 1862.

The second section of this act authorized the Secretary to cause the notes to be engraved and printed under his direction at the Treasury Department in Washington. The organization of a force for this purpose was prompt. From the employment of one male and four female operatives, this force grew into a bureau employing, at times, as many as eighteen hundred persons. Hardly had the organization taken shape when scandal began to attach to it, and in consequence there was no lack of investigation by Congress and the Secretary. For many years it was hardly ever free from an investigation of some kind. Extravagant appropriations were made by Congress for its maintenance, and, to keep the unnecessary employees busy the officers of the bureau established an elaborate and unnecessary system of checks and balances. The bureau opened wide its doors to the patronage of any person supposed to have influence in securing appropriations for its benefit; consequently it soon partook somewhat of the character of a parish alms-house, and a general retreat for dependents of politicians, and continued so until Secretary Sherman, in 1877, with a strong arm cleaned up the establishment, returned to the Treasury an unnecessary appropriation for it of nearly half a million, secured for it a proper building, organized its force for business only, and took it out of the domain of the caucus and the church, the powers which had before controlled it.

The policy of employing women in the public departments originated in this bureau, being another innovation in the conduct of public business resulting from the use of United States notes. The notes were printed in New York, and came in sheets from the printer, and women were employed to cut them apart and to trim them for circulation. Subsequently this work came to be done by machinery, and the women were transferred elsewhere to copy letters, to count notes and stamps, and to fill other positions.

Congress assembled in December, 1862, to legislate for a country wounded almost unto death in the house of those who had been its friends. To re-fill the armies at the front, decimated by unsuccessful struggles in the field and by the fevers of the camp, the government, as a last resort, had applied a relentless draft. The public treasury was empty, and the pay of the soldiers in arrears. The public credit was at a lower ebb than ever before in the history of the country. The six per cent twenty-year bonds of the government were freely offered in the market at the rate of $100 in bonds for $65 in gold; and of the legal-tender notes $100 could be exchanged for $68 of gold.

Secretary Chase pressed upon Congress, with much zeal and great ability, his scheme for organizing the national banking system, but admitted at the same time that at best not much, if any, relief from that source could be expected within a year; and again recommended, among other projects to meet temporary emergencies, the issue of additional United States notes. The notes at that time being worth more than an equal amount of six per cent bonds, the holders would not present them for conversion at par, and to make the notes less valuable, so that their conversion into bonds would surely follow, he recommended that the authority to thus convert them be taken away. In this way he could, with additional issues, depress their value to almost any extent he desired.

He argued that, if paper money was in excess of the notes of the country, such excess was not due to the issue of United States notes, but to the issue of notes by the State banks, which, without restriction, had flooded the country. That the advance in the price of gold was not due to over-issues of United States notes, but that gold, being practically demonetized by the suspension of the banks, had become a mere article of merchandise, subject to fluctuations such as might occur in other commodities. He thought, however, that these notes were not in excess, because as much of the great staples of life could be bought with them as with an equivalent of gold, before that metal disappeared from circulation.

The banks, it is true, had increased somewhat their circulation, as they had a right to do, but they compelled no one to take their notes, which could not be said of the government, whose printing-presses were in competition with those of the banks. Reference to the price-list for commodities of that period clearly shows that the notes possessed no such purchasing power as he asserted.

Congress acted promptly. On the 8th of December Mr. Stevens introduced in the House a bill to provide ways and means to support the government. Subsequently he said the bill had "produced a howl among the money-changers as hideous as that sent forth by their Jewish cousins when they were kicked out of the temple." Well it might. The bill proposed to issue $200,000,000 of legal tenders, $1,000,000,000 of six per cent bonds, and to tax the State banks out of existence. With some modification it became a law March 3, 1863.

This act authorized the issue, as the exigencies of the service might require, of $150,000,000 more of United States notes, in every way of like character to those already issued. Also an amount, not to exceed $400,000,000 of notes payable at the pleasure of the government, as might be found most beneficial to public interest, not to exceed three years, and to bear interest not to exceed six per cent in lawful money, and to be issued in denominations of not less than ten dollars, and to be a legal tender for their face value to the same extent as the United States notes.

In addition to the amount of United States notes issued under the authority of this act, there was issued of one-year notes, bearing interest at five per cent, $44,520,000, and of two-year notes, bearing interest at six per cent, $166,480,000..

By another provision of this act, the time when any of the United States notes could be converted at par into six per cent bonds was limited to the July 1, 1863, and a duty of two per cent a year was levied upon the circulation of the State banks.

No other legal tender notes were issued by the government during the civil war. By the provisions of an act approved June 30, 1864, however, authority was given for the issue of Treasury notes, bearing interest, payable at maturity or at the discretion of the Secretary, and of the amount issued those made payable, principal and interest, *at maturity*, if any, should be a legal tender. Except to the extent they furnished the legal reserve for national banks, thus liberating United States notes for circulation, they can hardly be treated as a part of the circulation of the country.

Authority being given by law to reissue indefinitely any of the United States notes mentioned, no care has been taken, in reissuing them, to maintain any distinction in the character of the notes issued, and no one can tell to-day under which of the acts authorizing such notes any one of them has been issued. The amount outstanding at one time has, however, never exceeded the aggregate amount authorized to be issued by the three acts, the highest amount having been January 30, 1864, when it reached $449,338,902. The total amount of legal tender paper issued by the government, under these acts, may be thus stated:

Demand notes	$60,030,000
United States notes	449,338,902
One-year five per cent notes	44,520,000
Compound interest notes	266,505,440
Two-year six per cent notes	166,480,000

These notes were never all outstanding at any one time. On the 31st of August, 1865, when the public debt reached its highest point, Secretary McCulloch reported the following legal tender items in his summing up of the debt of that date:

United States notes	$433,160,569
Five per cent notes	33,954,230
Compound interest notes	217,024,160
Total	$684,138,959

It is doubtful if the legal tender paper of the government outstanding at one date to that time ever exceeded that limit. The 7/30 notes issued under the act of June 30, 1864, had upon them yearly coupons; consequently they were only loans, and they bore no legend indicating that they possessed any legal tender quality, and they never circulated as money.

CHAPTER XIV.

FALLACY OF LEGISLATION.

Mr. Chase, because of disagreements growing out of the appointment of assistant treasurer at New York, left the treasury June 7, 1864. The dollar was then worth thirty-five cents in coin, and the loans, nominally selling at par in paper, were in fact being put on the market at sixty-five per cent discount. The Secretary, although not required by law to dispose of the loans at par in paper, evidently believed it bad policy to sell them at a discount, otherwise impertinent inquiries might be made concerning the boasted value of the notes. The loans, however, were worth only what purchasers would give for them in other commodities, no more and no less. Congress might, by the exercise of a doubtful power, compel a creditor to accept less in satisfaction of a debt than the contract called for, or it might, under its constitutional prerogative to regulate the value of money, force upon the country a medium whose exchange value for other commodities fluctuated violently from day to day; but to the owner of commodities it could not say at what rate he should part with them.

These commodities, which through many prosperous years had been accumulating throughout the country, were estimated to have an exchange value equivalent to $16,000,000,000 of coin, and the owners of these vast accumulations were in fact the government itself, and it was their own representatives who were calling for aid to make this wealth available to carry on the war.

The government had three practical methods:

First, to seize commodities wherever found, by force, and then to convert them by exchange into the form desired.

Second, to impose a tax by which the owners of the commodities should be compelled to deliver a portion of their gains from time to time as needed.

Third, to borrow the commodities with promises to return an equivalent at some specified time with proper compensation for their use.

Any one of these methods was proper, manly, and honest.

The first, however, was not to be thought of except in extreme necessity. The second, though a fair method, would, if carried beyond a certain limit, be unpopular even among the most patriotic. The third, though requiring time and "shinning" through the streets to affect negotiations, was the most expedient.

The government levied a tax to meet a small portion of its needs, and undertook to borrow for the remainder. For a year or so it was successful. Through the banks and other fiscal agencies owners of wealth were reached, and were induced to part with their commodities in exchange for government promises, at not unreasonable rates. The law of supply and demand fixed the rates as it does in other exchanges.

As the war progressed, however, doubts began to be entertained whether the government would be able to fulfil its promises as they matured, — in fact, whether there would be any government left for that or any other purpose; consequently holders of wealth declined to part with it except on terms commensurate with the increased risk. The supply of commodities, at the same time, grew less as the demand increased, and the rates of exchange at best were naturally somewhat enhanced. If the government continued to borrow it must do so only upon less favorable terms than had before existed. The owners of commodities had an undoubted right to exact the best terms they could obtain, and there was no alternative left for the government but to accept the best rates obtainable.

To do this, however, was regarded by many as humiliating to the national pride, and so a loan was attempted, to be negotiated in this way: The government, in exchange for commodities desired, gave to the lender a paper saying to him, in effect, "Here is my note for the amount due; it has no specified time for payment, it bears no interest, but take it, and if you don't think it is good make haste to trade it off on the first person you meet, and the faster you run the less you will lose." The lender was, however, generally prepared for the proposition, and he rated his commodities so high that even with this note taken in payment he could replace them at a profit.

Some, however, were not as vigilant; and it is related of one merchant that he sold to the government a hogshead of sugar at twenty per cent advance on cost, receiving these notes in payment. With the notes received he bought another hogshead, and sold this with a like advance, and repeated the operation until he had neither the notes nor sugar left; although he thought he was all the time accumulating wealth. He may have thought that the sugar was exchanged for value, but he might as well have made it a gift to the government at once, and thus saved time and trouble.

Secretary Chase, members of Congress, and many others believed that in issuing such notes the country was benefited; that for nothing it had obtained something, and some went so far as to think that wealth was created by such issues.

They did not know that with the sixth day the labor of creation ended, and some there be who have not learned it yet.

The policy of issuing these notes has been justified on several grounds:

First, the notes were a necessity.

Doubtless in the winter of 1861–2 the government was sorely pressed for means to carry on its operations. Its credit was untarnished, however, and subsequent events showed there was ample wealth in the country to meet all the demands necessary. The government had only to levy a proper tax, and then to exchange its credit, the only commodity it possessed, for what it needed, at the best rate obtainable. This rate might seem like extortion, but there was no help for it, and it was not avoided by the issue of the notes.

Second, the notes enabled the government to obtain money without begging for it.

The notes themselves were a loan as much as though they had coupons attached to them, but they had one advantage over other loans. The government could not only exchange them for commodities, but it could impose them at par upon the soldiers in the field, and upon other persons in its employ whose compensation had been fixed by law; and debtors generally could pay obligations with them to the extent of an equal amount of coin. The difference between the face value of the notes at the time of their issue in payment of salaries and their value in coin was a gain to the government, and to that extent the government was benefited, but no further. To compensate the soldier for the depreciation in the value of the notes his pay was increased, so that even in his case the government gained little. In purchasing supplies for forces in the field it paid prices commensurate with the depreciation of the notes. From a table carefully prepared in the treasury department, it appears that for the year 1864 the average coin price in New York of the leading commodities was twelve per cent above that of the same commodities in 1861, and that $110.10 in coin had an average purchasing power for 1864 equal to $223.80 in paper. The average price of $100 of gold for that year, measured in paper, as shown by other official publications, was $203.30, or, in other words, $1.00 in gold was worth $2.03 of paper. If a purchaser then, with $110.10 in gold, had converted it into paper at that rate he would have had $223.50, almost precisely the amount required to make it of equal purchasing power with gold. There could, therefore, be no possible gain in using these notes, and coin, or its equivalent, might as well have been employed at the outset.

Third, the notes helped to float the loan.

The loans were exchanged for commodities at

the best rates obtainable, — no better and no worse,—and the notes had no more to do with floating them than had the Atlantic Ocean. It is true the bonds were exchanged for the notes dollar for dollar, but when owners of the notes declined to part with them at that rate more notes were issued until the value was so depreciated that a bond would be accepted for them at par. Mention has already been made of an instance where the right to exchange these notes for six per cent bonds at par was taken away, so that the Secretary could force down the price of the notes until the owners would be willing to accept for them even a five per cent bond at par. In this way and no other did the notes float the loan. Had the notes been issued for coin the government would have received precisely the same equivalent, the gold having a purchasing power correspondingly great. Instead of the notes facilitating the issue of loans, there is every reason to believe that the government could have obtained better rates for its credit if the notes had never been issued. Undoubtedly the great cause for the depreciation of the bonds was the doubt existing as to the result of the struggle with the rebellion. There should have been no other cause. Of wealth to meet the payment of the loan at maturity there was an abundance in the country, and until the issue of these notes there had been no occasion to question the good faith of the government in all its monetary transactions; and integrity in a government as well as in a person has a commercial value.

Unfortunately, however, the several acts under which the loans of the government were issued did not state in what kind of dollars the bonds would be paid when they became due. Many persons asserted that, as the notes were a legal tender in the payment of all debts public and private, the holders of matured bonds would be compelled to accept the notes therefor, whatever might be their depreciation, and as the law especially specified that the interest on the loans was to be paid in coin, there seems strong reasons for such assertions. Doubts of this kind could not but affect the exchange value of the loans, and they did. The purchaser of the bonds had calculated the chances of military success, and parted with his commodities at a rate which he believed was justified by the risks assumed. But when the character of the money in which the payment of the bonds at maturity was to be made became questionable, there entered into his reckoning another element of doubt, making the purchase of the bond a lottery in which the purchaser had against him success in arms and integrity in legislation. To buy a government bond under such conditions was like purchasing a pool on a horse-race when the record of the horses was unknown and little confidence felt in the integrity of the jockeys. Under such circumstances investors demanded, and the government had to give, large odds. Thus the notes, instead of floating the loans, helped to depress them.

Fourth, the notes furnished a uniform circulating medium.

When the civil war broke out the government had a uniform circulating medium of gold coin, supplemented by bank-notes substantially circulating at par with gold. The gold was a medium uniform throughout the civilized world, and being everywhere recognized for what it was worth could maintain its uniformity of value without adventitious aid. The introduction of these notes drove the gold from circulation and depreciated the value of the bank-notes. In less than a year after their issue the notes had an exchange value for other commodities less by thirty per cent than when originally issued, and they fluctuated violently from day to day, all the time growing of less and less value, until a witty member of Congress suggested an increase in rate of duty on paper and dye stuffs, so that in case of further issue the notes might not become wholly worthless. The notes destroyed a uniform circulating medium, and such a medium was not restored until the resumption of 1879, when the notes themselves became redeemable in coin.

They were never uniform except in their variations of value.

Fifth, the notes had an additional value from their legal tender quality.

At the outbreak of the rebellion there was in circulation $180,000,000 of bank issues, and an estimated amount of $250,000,000 in coin, in all about $430,000,000. We have before seen that money left to itself will always equal the precise amount needed to effect the exchanges of products. As gold was the medium circulating in Europe, any excess in this country in 1861 would have gone there until the equilibrium of circulation between the countries was restored. None went, but in fact a small amount came into the country from Europe in that year, indicating that the amount in circulation here had somewhat passed the minimum limit and was being restored. We have also seen that if a circulating medium becomes excessive through artificial restraint, prices of commodities will be correspondingly raised. If two dollars exist where there is a demand for only one, nobody will give of his commodities for both dollars more than he would for one, there being, practically, no use for the extra dollar. Whether the circulating medium is gold, silver, copper, or paper the same rule is true.

In 1861 the business of this country required in making exchanges about $430,000,000 in gold coin, or equivalents thereto. In 1864 gold coin had been supplanted by legal tender issues, the face value of which averaged for that year about $840,000,000, and this amount had an average value for the year, in gold, of about $420,000,000. In addition thereto gold was maintained in circulation in California, and enough of it in ports of entry to meet custom duties. But on the other hand, in 1864 eleven States, having a portion of the circulation in 1861, were in rebellion, and a fair estimate would indicate that on the whole there had been no especial demand in 1864 for an increased circulating medium. In 1864 the exchange, and not the face, value of the notes, fixed with an inexorable law the amount of them which could be maintained in circulation. As notes depreciated, more of them, in amount, could be made to circulate, but this increase was owing to their decreased value, not to any extraordinary quality with which the notes were endowed. Four hundred and twenty millions of gold, or its equivalent, was the amount of circulation the country required in 1864. The issue of notes furnished this amount, and no more. Other circumstances fixed the value of the notes, and business accepted them for circulation at the rate thus fixed. Had there been no issue of notes, coin, or its equivalent in convertible paper, would have continued to do duty. There was an abundance of coin in the country for this purpose. When Secretary Chase asked the banks where he could get coin to carry on the war, what he wanted was wealth, not coin, since the latter would come of itself, when needed, if not prevented by legislation.

The owner of legal tender notes, however, could not only exchange them for commodities, but he could with them pay debts; and their use for this purpose might possibly give them a little additional value over that of notes not enjoying a legal tender quality, but the bank notes of the country, which no one was obliged to receive for any purpose, circulated at par with United States notes, and so strongly competed for favor that the government taxed them out of existence. The demand notes of the government, before endowed with a legal tender quality, circulated generally at par with gold, maintaining a higher rate than that ever reached by the legal tender notes until their redeemability was secured. The United States notes circulated at a discount until within three days of the time of redeemability, in itself an indication of the futility of effort of the government to give to the notes a value which would not be recognized by the laws of commerce and trade.

CHAPTER XV.

NATIONAL BANK ISSUES.

In 1861 sixteen hundred banks, organized and operated under the widely differing laws of the several States, provided the greater part of the currency of the country. Their issues aggregated at that time about $200,000,000, their deposits $250,000,000 — a total immediate liability of $450,000,000, to meet which there was held about $116,000,000 of specie, or its equivalent. The loans outstanding aggregated about $700,000,000, while the capital stock was about $430,000,000. Of the capital $110,000,000, and of the circulation of $50,000,000, were in the seceding States.

The circulating notes were far from satisfactory. Except in the amount of the reserve held against them, the banks had a clear profit in their issue, and generally the weaker the bank the greater was its effort to sustain itself by an excessive issue. The notes of even the stronger banks were subject to more or less discount, as they were far from, or near to, the place of issue. Chicago bills were at a discount in New York, and New York bills at a discount in Chicago of sometimes as high as five per cent. A traveller between the two cities, with a capital of $1,000, could pay travelling expenses by a judicious trading of bills, buying the depreciated bills in one city to be disposed of at par in the other. A conductor on a "through" train would often refuse bills outright at one point of the line which he received at par at another. The use of bank-note detectors was necessary in order to ascertain the genuineness of notes, and the solvency, or the existence even, of the banks of which they purported to be the issue.

The inferior quality of the paper on which the bills were printed, and the imperfections in the printing itself, made counterfeiting easy and its detection difficult. Trustworthy reports from eighteen different States show that in 1860, out of twelve hundred and thirty banks, one hundred and forty were broken, two hundred and thirty-four closed, and one hundred and thirty-one worthless. There were in existence at that time three thousand kinds of altered notes, seventeen hundred varieties of spurious notes, four hundred and sixty varieties of imitation, and over seven hundred of other kinds more or less fraudulent. The various kinds of genuine bills in circulation were about seven thousand. If those who tampered with the notes were as industrious as were the bank officials in putting them into circulation, one might expect, by the law of chance, to find that out of every eleven notes in circulation five had been tampered with and that only six were genuine; but even the genuine ones were at par only near their respective places of issue.

After our experience of twenty years with the present currency, we can hardly realize the annoyances and loss to which the country was subjected by the circulation of such bills. The present currency, in its purchasing power, may fluctuate greatly, but one bill is as good as another of the same denomination, and wherever, or by whomsoever issued, is received at par everywhere in the country. The paper of which the notes are made is of the best quality, and of late years has been characterized by distinctive marks. The printing is done from steel plates of the highest order of the engraver's art, thus rendering counterfeiting difficult and the publication of detectors almost unnecessary. A portion of this currency is issued directly by the government, and the remainder by the national banks, which have, in issuing bills, wholly supplanted the State banks.

The first suggestion of the national banking system appears to have come from Secretary Chase. Thinking at once to get rid of the objectionable issues of the State banks, and to substitute therefor a currency which would protect holders from loss, and at the same time enable the government to obtain means for prosecuting the war, he submitted to Congress, on the 9th day of December, 1861, two plans for effecting the object.

One plan contemplated the withdrawal from circulation of all the State bank notes, and the issue in their stead of United States notes payable in coin on demand, in amount sufficient to meet the wants of a representative currency. The other plan contemplated the preparation and delivery to institutions and associations, of notes prepared for circulation under a national direction, and secured, as to prompt convertibility into coin, by a pledge of United States bonds and by needful regulations.

The first of these plans had already been partially adopted by the issue of demand notes, and had the issue of these notes been extended gradually, with a proper reserve to maintain their redeemability in coin, and had the State banks been imperatively required to keep their issues at par in coin, the country would have had a currency as creditable and profitable, perhaps, as any form of credit issues.

But to Mr. Chase this plan presented inconvenience and hazard. He feared that the temptation to issue notes beyond adequate provision for redemption would not be resisted, and that there would thence arise "the immeasurable evils of dishonored public faith and national bankruptcy," and that possible disasters which might result therefrom would far outweigh any possible benefit. He therefore proposed a second plan, which, in brief, was : —

1st. The circulation of notes bearing a common impression, and authenticated by common authority.

2d. The redemption of these notes by the associations and institutions to which they might be delivered.

3d. The security of the redemption by a pledge of United States stocks, and an adequate provision of specie.

He believed that the notes thus issued and secured would form the safest currency the country had ever enjoyed; that being receivable, as he thought they should be, for all public dues except customs, they would be of equal value as currency in every part of the United States; that the large amount of specie in the country, estimated at $275,000,000, would easily support payment of duties in coin, and that with such payments, and with the ordinary demand, the specie would stay in the country, as a solid basis both for circulation and loans.

He expressed great confidence in the plan because it was not wholly an untried one. In the State of New York, and perhaps in other States, it had been subjected to the test of experience, and found practicable and safe. He also thought that existing solvent institutions would substitute these notes for their own, that the notes of weaker banks would disappear, and that the government would be greatly benefited by the sale of bonds, to be issued as a basis of circulation.

Such was the scheme presented to Congress by Secretary Chase in December, 1861. It met with but little favor. In less than two months thereafter Congress was discussing the policy of issuing legal tender notes with no provision for their redemption, and was endeavoring to drag the Secretary into its support as a last resort for obtaining means to carry on the war. It is worthy of note that on the 9th day of December the Secretary saw no necessity for suspending specie payments, and shrank from such a contingency; yet at the same time that he was thus opposing their issue, he was pushing the demand notes into circulation, and forcing the suspension which came at the end of the month.

The issue of United States notes under the act of February 25, 1862, bridged over the existing financial embarrassments, and Congress adjourned without considering the proposed plan for a national banking system.

Upon the re-assembling of Congress, in December following, Mr. Chase, in his annual report, renewed his recommendation of a system of national banks, and reinforced it with strong arguments. He again expressed his conviction that, while government notes were preferable to the issue of State banks, the circulation to be furnished by national banks, as he had recommended, would be better than either. He recognized the cheapness of government notes and their facility of production in times of emergency, but on the other hand thought that there would be danger of excessive expansion, which would be accompanied by lavish and corrupt expenditure.

The associations he proposed were to be voluntary, but as a bounty he would impose a tax on the issues of the State banks. Their establishment would give every person holding a dollar of their circulation an interest in the preservation of the government, upon whose credit the notes were issued, and thus out of the public debt, though never of itself a good, this benefit might be extracted.

At the close of the previous Congress this measure was, as we have seen, almost friendless. Representative Hooper, of Boston, almost alone favored it in the House. The State banks were almost unanimously opposed to it. Rankling memories of the old United States Bank were everywhere revived, and the proposed repression of the State issues and the substitution of notes issued by associations organized under authority of the general government were measures especially obnoxious to Democratic congressmen. But meanwhile the measure had evidently gained in popularity, and a bill embodying the scheme recommended by the Secretary was promptly introduced in the Senate and exhaustively debated. Mr. Collamer summed up the chief objections against it. They were : —

That it proposed to tax State banks out of existence. That it substituted for the State banks then doing business at least three thousand, and perhaps six thousand institutions, entirely independent of the power of visitation by the States. That the capital employed would not be subject to State taxation. That it made the government responsible for the ultimate redemption of the circulation to be issued. That it put great political power into the hands of the Secretary of the Treasury. That it hired the banking associations, at a yearly expense of $12,000,000 in gold, to circulate $300,000,000 of currency among the people, who were at last responsible for its redemption. In short, that the people of the country would derive no benefit from the operations of the bill, and that after all the profits derived to the banks would be very small.

To this Mr. Sherman replied that if $100,000,000 of the circulation of the State banks were withdrawn, the government would reap an advantage, at any rate, of a market for $100,000,000 of its stocks, and that the creation of the demand for $100,000,000 would excite a further demand for $500,000,000. That the power of the Secretary would be weakened rather than strengthened by the operation of the proposed system, inasmuch as the powers conferred by the bill were more likely to make enemies than friends for the Secretary who exercised them.

The bill passed both houses. In the Senate the vote stood 23 for, and 21 against it; in the House 78 for, and 64 against it. One Democratic senator — Nesmith of Oregon — voted for the bill, and seven Republican senators voted against it. In the House two Democrats voted for it, and twenty-five Republicans against it. It became a law February 25, 1863.

The act provided for an additional bureau in the Treasury Department charged with the execution of the law, the chief officer of which was to be denominated "The Comptroller of the Currency."

The principal features of the bill relating to the issue of notes were these: —

Thirty per cent of the capital stock was to be paid in before the bank could begin business. As a preliminary to the beginning of business an association was required to transfer and deliver to the United States Treasurer interest-bearing bonds of the United States, in amount not less than one-third of the capital stock paid in, whereupon it was entitled to receive from the Comptroller circulating notes of various denominations in blank, but registered and countersigned at the department, equal to ninety per cent of the current value of the bonds, but not exceeding their par value.

The whole amount of circulation authorized was $300,000,000, of which one half was to be apportioned according to population, the other half according to the then existing banking capital, resources, and business of the States, Territories, and District of Columbia.

To reimburse the expense of the government in preparing the notes, a tax of two per cent per annum was imposed upon the amount of the circulation of the associations in lieu of all other taxes upon the notes and the security bonds.

The notes were made receivable in payment of all dues to the United States except duties on imports, and payable in satisfaction of all demands against the United States, except interest on the public debt.

Every association was required to have on hand at all times, in lawful money of the United States, a sum equal to twenty-five per cent of the aggregate of its outstanding circulation and deposits.

No association was to pay out or put in circulation the notes of any bank or banking association, which should not be receivable at the time at par, on deposit or in payment of debts due the assotion paying out or circulating them. Nor could it circulate the notes of any association which did not at that time redeem its notes in the lawful money of the United States. Provision was also made for the conversion of State banks into these associations.

Secretary Chase, in his next annual report, Dec. 10, 1863, ascribed salutary effects to the operation of the act. Up to that time 134 banks had been organized, chiefly in the west, with an aggregate capital of $16,000,000. Some defects in the act had naturally been developed in the year's experience of its practical working, to correct which he recommended several amendments.

The debate upon the amendatory act developed all that could be urged against the system, to wit:—

1st. That it inflated the currency and raised prices.

2d. That it provided for an irredeemable currency.

3d. That it relieved the capital of the associations from State taxations.

In answer to the first allegation, that prices of commodities had largely increased, no denial could be made, but it was alleged that the increase was no more due to the expansion of bank circulation than to the issue of United States notes, and that the evils at best were but temporary and would disappear with success in the field.

Nor could the second allegation be denied, but it was alleged that after the suspension of the banks in 1861 a coin circulation was not believed possible, and that the government had to choose between the two paper currencies offered, one by the State banks also irredeemable in coin, which currency could be expanded and depreciated without restriction, the profits accruing to the banks issuing it; or one furnished by the government under its own direction and control, secured by the pledged faith of the United States, the profits of which should be for the benefit of the whole people of the country.

In reply to the third objection it was urged that, under the decisions of the Supreme Court, banks chartered by the United States could not be taxed by the State authorities, even without a special exemption therefrom by law, and the same was true as to the bonds and stocks of the government, and that for the benefit which might arise from the circulation the banks paid the government a generous tax.

The amendatory tax passed the Senate, only two Republicans voting against it, and none of the Democrats voting for it. In the House no Republican voted against it, and no Democrat voted for it. The bill became a law June 3, 1864. The amendments affecting the circulation were mainly these: —

1st. There was to be no restriction as to the distribution of the circulation, the aggregate amount, however, to remain at $300,000,000.

2d. The tax on circulation was reduced to one half of one per centum semi-annually, and a tax was imposed upon the deposits, and upon the capital stock in excess of the amount represented by bonds pledged to secure the circulating notes.

3d. Any association wishing to close its business could deliver to the Treasurer of the United States lawful money to the amount of its outstanding notes, and be entitled to receive therefor the return of the bonds pledged for their security.

By subsequent legislation, changes have been made, so that the banks can, at the present time, receive of circulating notes but ninety per centum of the face value of the pledged bonds, and they are not otherwise restricted as to the limit or distribution of their circulation.

In lieu of any reserve for circulation, every bank is now required to keep in the Treasury of the United States five per centum of the amount of its circulation; and the Treasurer is required to redeem therewith any notes of the bank presented for that purpose. If the bank issuing the redeemed notes is still doing business, new notes are issued to it in lieu of those redeemed and destroyed, and the five per cent fund must be reimbursed to that extent.

Every bank can also, at its discretion, decrease the amount of its circulation by depositing with the Treasurer of the United States legal-tender notes to the amount of the reduction contemplated. The Treasurer, upon receipt of the deposit, returns to the bank a corresponding amount of its security bonds, and redeems the notes of the bank to the extent of the deposit when they come into his possession. No limit is fixed to the time during which the notes of banks which have closed business must be presented for redemption, and, as a result, many notes will be worn out or otherwise destroyed, and will never be presented for redemption. No provision as to the disposition of the fund provided for the redemption of such destroyed notes has been made.

The fund deposited with the Treasurer for the redemption of notes of banks which have failed, gone into liquidation, or are reducing circulation, reaches at times nearly $50,000,000. This amount, whatever it may be, lies idle in the Treasury vaults.

Of this system of circulation much good can be said. No holder of a national bank-note has ever lost a cent through the failure of the bank issuing it; nor has he been subjected to a vexatious discount in passing it. Everywhere throughout the country the note passes at par, and no scrutiny is required to ascertain the place of its issue. Counterfeit issues are almost unknown,— so rare, indeed, that no one takes any precaution to guard against them. There is no monopoly in the system. Ten persons in any city having less than twenty-thousand inhabitants can organize a bank by contributing $5,000 each, one-half down, the remainder in easy instalments, and have whatever profits they can find in issuing circulating notes.

It is true that at first the national-bank notes, being made redeemable in lawful money of the United States, did not circulate at par in coin, but that time is happily passed, and hereafter no bank should be permitted, under any circumstances, to refuse payment of its notes in specie at par.

Opposition to the system has almost entirely disappeared throughout the land. From no source come any complaints of its operations, and in the United States Senate in 1883 no reply was elicited, no denial made, when one of its ablest members, a Democrat from Kentucky, remarked, "The national banks are out of politics. There is nobody making war upon them, nor are they, as such, interfering in political affairs. We need their circulation for a growing country, and therefore it will be a benefit for us all to maintain it."

CHAPTER XVI.

CONTRACTION.

At the close of the civil war the State banks had a circulation of $143,000,000, but a law imposing a tax of ten per cent upon the amount of the notes of such banks paid out by any banking association took effect on the first day of July, 1865, and there could be but one result, — the issues of State banks must go. The national banks at that time had issued but $146,000,000 of the $300,000,000 authorized. The government had outstanding $433,000,000 of United States notes, $217,000,000 of compound-interest notes, $34,000,000 of five per cent notes, and $25,000,000 of fractional notes. The total amount of paper currency outstanding was $983,000,000, having a coin value of $692,000,000, the coin value of the paper dollar being seventy-one cents.

Fiscal Year 1866.

Secretary McCulloch, in his annual report for 1865, expressed the opinion that the issue of legal tender notes, being a war measure, a temporary expedient adopted in a great emergency; they ought not to remain in use longer than was necessary to enable the people to return to a gold standard, and that the work of retiring the notes which had been issued should be commenced without delay and carefully and persistently continued until all were retired. The House of Representatives on December 18, 1865, under a suspension of the rules, by a vote of one hundred and forty-four yeas to six nays, resolved: —

"That this House cordially concurs in the views of the Secretary in relation to the necessity of a contraction of the currency, with a view to as early a resumption of specie payment as the business interests of the country will permit, and we hereby pledge co-operative action to this end as speedily as possible."

To carry out this policy, Congress, by an act approved April 12, 1866, directed: "That of United States notes not more than $10,000,000 may be retired and cancelled within six months from the passage of this act, and thereafter not more than $4,000,000 in any one month."

On the date of the approval of this act there were outstanding of United States notes $422,000,000. At the close of the fiscal year, June 30, 1866, the circulation of State banks had decreased $141,000,000, that of United States notes $33,000,000, the amount of compound-interest notes $143,000,000, and that of the one and two year notes $40,000,000, while the circulation of the national-bank notes had increased but $135,000,000.

It may be alleged that the interest-bearing notes had passed entirely out of circulation. In one sense this allegation is true, — they were no longer used in making exchanges; but being a legal tender for their face value they furnished, and were used as, a lawful reserve for the national banks, taking the place of United States notes to the extent that they were thus used, and swelling the aggregate circulation by a corresponding amount. Upon maturity, large amounts of them came back to the Treasury from the banks, with the seals of their original packages unbroken. Notwithstanding the great reduction in the paper circulation, the coin value of one dollar in paper was five cents less at the end of the year than at the beginning, — a poor encouragement for any plan of resumption by contracting the currency.

It should be remembered, however, that on June 30, 1865, a year before, a large army had just been disbanded and paid off, calling into use a large amount of circulating notes throughout the country; large sales of public stores and property were being made for cash, and these transactions caused a demand for circulation which did not exist in 1866. The total amount of paper circulation June 30, 1866, was $892,000,000, a reduction within the year of $9,500,000. The coin value of the circulation was, however, but $589,000,000, a reduction of $103,000,000 of coin valuation, the coin valuation of paper being sixty-six cents.

Fiscal Year 1867.

The Secretary continued his policy of retiring United States notes, as provided by law. The compound-interest notes were also being rapidly funded into five-twenty bonds, but the national banks meanwhile were increasing their issues. By the withdrawal of the interest-bearing notes the banks had to keep their reserve in non-productive money, and they made an earnest appeal to Congress for relief. This relief was partly granted. Congress, by an act approved March 2, 1867, authorized a temporary loan of $50,000,000 in the form of certificates, bearing three per cent interest per annum; the proceeds to be used in the redemption of the compound-interest notes; the certificates issued to be used as a lawful reserve for the banks. They were thus used, and any reduction during that year in the amount of United States notes was more than offset by the issue of this loan. Notwithstanding the issue of the three per cent certificates, the aggregate amount outstanding of interest-bearing notes rapidly decreased, and there was no means by which the aggregate circulation could be increased, the circulation of the banks having already reached the limit authorized by law. The amount of outstanding paper circulation June 30, 1867, was $827,000,000, having a coin value of $587,000,000, a decrease during the year in face value of $65,000,000, but a decrease in coin value of only $2,000,000. The paper dollar now had a coin value of seventy-one cents, an increase during the year of five cents.

Fiscal Year 1868.

Upon the assembling of Congress in December, 1867, there was a threatened stringency in the money market. A considerable decline in the prices of commodities had already taken place, the country was on the road to resumption at last, but the wrecks of fortunes threatened to strew its pathway. Congress became alarmed and determined to postpone the evils it could not avoid. On February 4, 1868, the authority to further retire United States notes was suspended, leaving outstanding $356,000,000. On June 30, 1868, there remained outstanding of compound-interest notes only $28,000,000, but the issues of three per cent certificates had increased to $50,000,000. Including the amount of these certificates, the total paper circulation at that date was $770,000,000, having a coin value of $540,000,000, a reduction during the year of $57,000,000 in face value and of $47,000,000 in coin value. The paper dollar was now worth seventy cents in coin, one cent less than it was a year before, notwithstanding the large reduction in the aggregate amount of circulation.

Fiscal Year 1869.

On July 25, 1868, Congress, in order to favor the banks and to avoid a possible stringency in the money market, authorized an additional issue of $25,000,000 of the three per cent certificates. A new question now arose and had to be met. In several of the acts authorizing the issue of United States bonds the character of the currency in which they were to be paid at maturity was left in doubt, and a determined effort was made by a large class of people, especially by those who had not been friendly to the purposes of the war, to secure the payment of these loans in the notes for which they were issued. Congress, however, by an act approved March 18, 1869, set these questions at rest by declaring that the faith of the United States was solemnly pledged to the payment, in coin or its equivalent, of all the obligations of the United States not bearing interest, known as United States notes, and all the interest-bearing obligation of the United States, except in cases where the law authorizing the issue of any such obligations had expressly provided that the same might be paid in lawful money or other currency than gold or silver. And it also pledged the faith of the United States to provide at the earliest practicable period for the redemption of United States notes in coin. This act had the effect of strengthening the public credit and of increasing the value of United States notes. Including the amount of these three per cent certificates, the aggregate amount of outstanding circulation at the close of the fiscal year ending June 30, 1869, was $756,000,000, having a coin value of $552,000,000, a decrease of $14,000,000 in face value and an increase of $12,000,000 in coin value. The paper dollar was now worth in coin seventy-three cents, a gain during the year of three cents.

Fiscal Year 1870.

On June 30, 1870, the aggregate of paper circulation was $745,000,000, having a coin value of $633,000,000, a decrease during the year of $11,000,000 in its face value, but an increase of $81,000,000 in its coin value. A dollar in paper was now worth eighty-five cents, a gain in value during the year of twelve cents..

Fiscal Year 1871.

On the 12th of July, 1870, an act was approved

authorizing an additional issue of $54,000,000 national bank circulation, an equivalent amount of three per cent certificates to be redeemed; and on June 30, 1871, the banks had increased their circulation to $418,000,000. The aggregate circulation at this date was $748,000,000, with a coin value of $665,000,000, a paper dollar being now worth eighty-nine cents, an increase within the year of four cents.

Fiscal Year 1872.

Another question now arose to agitate the country. The acts of Congress of February 25 and June 11, 1862, and March 3, 1863, had together authorized the issue of $400,000,000 of United States notes in addition to $50,000,000 of such notes reserved for the purpose of securing prompt payment of temporary loan deposits, and the act of June 30, 1864, contained these words: "Nor shall the total amount of United States notes, issued or to be issued, ever exceed $400,000,000, and such additional sum, not exceeding $50,000,000, as may be temporarily required for the redemption of temporary loans."

The temporary loans referred to having been redeemed, the maximum amount of United States notes was evidently fixed by the last-named act at $400,000,000.

The act of April 12, 1866, provided, as we have

seen, that a certain amount of United States notes might be retired and cancelled. The act of Feb. 4, 1868, provided that the authority to make any reduction of the currency by retiring and cancelling United States notes should thereafter be suspended. Between the dates of these two acts the amount outstanding of United States notes was reduced from $422,000,000 to $356,000,000, and as the notes withdrawn had been retired and cancelled, as provided by law, and reduced to ashes, as provided by Treasury regulations, they were generally supposed to have passed beyond the power of resurrection; but some financial genius discovered that the maximum limit of $400,000,000 to which the notes could be issued remained untouched, and that the Secretary of the Treasury had consequently a reserve of $44,000,000 of United States notes which he could issue and retire at his discretion. By virtue of this newly discovered discretionary power Secretary Boutwell, in October, 1871, to relieve a stringency in Wall Street, issued of this reserve $1,500,000.

At the end of the year, June 30, 1872, the amount of paper circulation was $738,000,000, the banks having increased their issues about $20,000,000. The coin value of this circulation was now $646,000,000, a paper dollar being worth eighty-seven cents and a half, a decrease in value during the year of one cent and a half, mainly brought about by the alarm which arose from the action of the Secretary in reissuing the notes.

Fiscal Year 1873.

The previous year ended with seeming prosperity throughout the country. In all parts labor met with good demand and remunerative compensation, and manufacturing enterprises were especially prosperous. The Secretary, at his discretion, had from time to time caused additional issues to be made from the alleged reserve, although his authority to do so was doubted by many. Even if the right to re-issue these notes existed, the necessity of exercising what at best was a doubtful and dangerous prerogative may be questioned. The receipts of the government were largely in excess of the expenditures, and bonds were being purchased with the surplus at a considerable premium. The public Treasury, at the same time, was strong, holding of cash more than $70,000,000 in excess of all matured demands outstanding.

The Secretary, in his annual report to Congress, made no reference to this important subject. The increased amount of the notes, however, appeared in the monthly debt statement and other official publications, and neither Congress nor the country was ignorant of their issue. Of this reserve there was issued in all $4,637,256, but the outcry against the policy was so strong that $3,481,541 was retired. Secretary Richardson, who succeeded Secretary Boutwell in March, 1873, immediately retired the remainder of the reserve issue, and at the close of the year, June 30, 1873, the amount outstanding was again reduced to $356,000,000. Meanwhile the banks had increased their issues to $347,000,000, and the amount of fractional currency which had been gradually increasing now reached more than $44,000,000.

The entire circulation June 30, 1873, was $750,000,000, coin value $648,000,000, the value of the paper dollar being eighty-six and a half cents, a still further depreciation of one cent.

Fiscal Year 1874.

Another year of intense activity in business had passed, the credit circulation of the country had been considerably increased, while the public debt had largely diminished, and there seemed to be no reason why this prosperous condition of affairs should not continue indefinitely. But suddenly in September, 1873, when the country was revelling in apparent prosperity, there came a crash. The country was roused from pleasant dreams to unpleasant realities. It was now seen that a million men in arms destroyed wealth instead of creating it; that goods manufactured beyond need were a drug in the market; that railroads built where there were neither passengers nor freight to carry could not pay dividends; that the values of commodities were not governed by the imagination of the owners; that men who habitually spent more than they earned would eventually become paupers, and generally that paying for the music did not give the ecstatic delight produced by the whirl of the dance.

The first indication of the approaching cyclone was the failure of a well-known banking house. The storm did not abate until all the industries of the country were wrecked or damaged. Failures in business were numerous on every hand, and the man in active business who could pay promptly the demands upon him was looked upon as a skinflint who had been devoid of enterprise and public spirit. Doubt and suspicion succeeded to hope and confidence. Men no longer dared to trust each other, and each one grasped all the money he could lay his hands on and kept it in his personal possession. The banks no longer received their customary deposits and consequently could with difficulty meet their obligations. With collateral of undoubted worth they could induce holders of money to part with their treasure only at exorbitant rates, if at all. The savings banks, although generally solvent, having extended their loans to the utmost limit to enable them to pay large dividends, were especially embarrassed to meet the demands of depositors, and their officers were forced into the streets to borrow money at ruinous rates in order to avoid the mortification of temporarily closing their doors.

In the vaults of the Treasury lay $50,000,000 of gold coin which could lawfully have been paid out in exchange for public obligations without embarrassing the operations of the government; but as specie could not be employed to pay private debts without a sacrifice at once of about twelve per cent, — the amount of its premium in paper, — it was not wanted. Nowhere else did there appear to be any accumulation of money, nor could the banks expand their issues, their maximum limit having already been reached. All eyes were therefore turned to the $44,000,000 note reserve lying in the Treasury, a portion of which had done duty in the previous year in an exigency far less pressing than this, and urgent demand arose for its issue. The Secretary yielded to this demand, and in exchange for public securities paid out $25,000,000 of it, thus affording a temporary relief to the embarrassed banks. For this action he was censured as well as praised. In his favor it can be said that for more than a year Congress had known that the Secretary claimed the right to issue and withdraw any portion of this reserve as circumstances might in his judgment require, and no steps had been taken to dispossess him of this extraordinary and dangerous power. Congress had also by its inaction needlessly left the country with only a local currency with which to effect exchanges. Gold, the currency of the world, was still only a commodity and unavailable for circulation. From the conditions indicated, only evils could flow in such a crisis, and the Secretary endeavored to make the evils as bearable as possible. Had the country been conducting its exchanges on a specie basis, no such crisis could have arisen. The gold of the Treasury would have met immediate wants, and for any additional needed amount European gold would have poured into Wall Street as soon as electricity could have invited it and steam brought it to our shores. Only by having the whole world for a market can a stringency of money be avoided in a panic like that of 1873.

Congress assembled in December following. The scarcity of money still continued to be severely felt throughout the country. The Secretary had from his reserve given relief to the banks, and men then asked "If banks can thus obtain relief, why not make the reserve large enough so that from it the government can relieve everybody and make money plentiful again?" The inquiry was pertinent and suggestive. The Senate crystallized the idea into a bill of two sections. The first section fixed the maximum limit of United States notes at $400,000,000; the second authorized $46,000,000 additional bank issues, and required each bank to retain as a part of its lawful reserve one-fourth part of the coin received by it as interest on the United States bonds deposited with the Treasurer of the United States to secure its circulation and deposits. The bill, however, prohibited any bank from keeping more than one-fourth part of its reserve in the banks of the reserve cities where the entire amount had usually been kept at a low rate of interest. Whether inflation or contraction would result from this measure nobody could tell. The friends of resumption opposed it, but were unable to defeat its passage. The President vetoed it, however, as an inflation measure, giving such cogent reasons for his action that even the promoters of the scheme had no reply to make. The influence of the action of the President had a gratifying effect throughout the country and called a halt to all inflation purposes.

On June 20, 1874, an act was approved fixing the issue of United States notes at $382,000,000, the amount then outstanding. The act also required every national bank to keep with the Treasurer of the United States five per cent of its circulation with which to redeem its notes, and required no other reserve for that purpose. The act also authorized any bank to reduce its circulation by depositing with the Treasurer for the redemption of its notes an amount of United States notes equal to the reduction proposed.

On June 30, 1874, the fiscal year ended with $781,000,000 of circulation outstanding, $46,000,000 being fractional notes; coin value $711,000,000; coin value of the paper dollar, ninety-one cents, a net gain during the year of four and a half cents, notwithstanding the increase in circulation of $31,000,000.

Fiscal Year 1875.

The distress following the panic of 1873 was not easily or quickly relieved, and Congress assembled in December, 1874, with the country looking to it for corrective legislation. The firmness of the President, as evinced in his veto measure of the preceding session, precluded any hope of further inflation of the currency and strengthened the hands of those who favored a return to specie payments. Early in the session a measure was reported to the Senate, commanding the support of the Republican side, and it was pressed through both houses as a purely partisan measure, no Democrat voting for it. It became a law Jan. 14, 1875, but its immediate effects were not encouraging. By the close of the fiscal year, June 30, 1875, the banks had increased their issues to $354,000,000 and the amount of United States notes was reduced to $375,000,000; total circulation $773,000,000, coin value $674,000,000, value of the paper dollar eighty-seven cents, a loss of four cents, notwithstanding the resumption act.

Fiscal Year 1876.

No further legislation affecting the issue of a credit circulation was adopted during this year. The banks, somewhat to the surprise of those who feared they might largely expand their issues, reported a decrease in the aggregate amount. New banks, however, had received issues which, under the provisions of the resumption act, required a corresponding reduction in the amount of United States notes. Contraction, therefore, resulted in both forms of credit circulation.

On June 30, 1876, the total circulation was $738,000,000, coin value $656,000,000, value of the paper dollar in coin eighty-nine cents, a gain of two cents, owing largely without doubt to a decreased circulation of $35,000,000.

Fiscal Year 1877.

During this year a large amount of fractional notes was redeemed by the issue in their place of fractional silver. The banks also continued to withdraw their circulation, and the volume of United States notes was considerably diminished. The circulation being now relieved of many restraints began to adjust itself to the needs of business, and good effects were felt. The total circulation, June 30, 1877, was $698,000,000, coin value $662,000,000, value of paper dollar ninety-five cents, a gain of six cents.

Fiscal Year 1878.

By the end of this year nearly all the fractional notes not destroyed had been redeemed in silver, only $16,000,000 remaining, of which only about $1,000,000 has since been redeemed. Congress contented itself with passing an act which was approved May 31, 1878, prohibiting the retirement of any more United States notes, and providing that when any such notes should thereafter be redeemed they should not be cancelled, but should be paid out again and kept in circulation. As no limit had ever been placed on the amount or kind of fund which the Secretary could keep on hand the last provision was of no possible consequence, but it pleased the opponents of resumption and at the same time did no harm. At the close of this year, June 30, 1878, the total amount of circulation was $688,000,000, coin value $684,000,000, value of a dollar in coin ninety-nine and a half cents. Resumption took place six months later, as provided by law.

To those who believe that the aggregate exchange value of a circulating medium can be increased or diminished by the will of Congress or any human agency is commended the fact that after sixteen years of legislative effort, by which the face value of the circulation was reduced more than $300,000,000, the coin value was reduced less than $6,000,000. The great law of demand

and supply fixed the amount needed and mocked the futile efforts of those who tried to overrule it.

The following statement shows in tabular form the changes which took place in the amount and valuation of the paper circulation for the years named: —

Statement showing the amount in millions of outstanding paper circulation and its value in coin, together with the value in coin of one dollar in paper, at the close of each fiscal year, from 1865 to 1879 inclusive.

Year ending June 30.	Amount of circulation. Millions.	Coin value of circulation. Millions.	Coin value of One Dollar of paper.
1865	$983	$697	$0.71
1866	892	589	0.66
1867	827	587	0.71
1868	770	540	0.70
1869	756	552	0.73
1870	745	633	0.85
1871	748	665	0.89
1872	738	646	0.87½
1873	750	648	0.86½
1874	781	711	0.91
1875	773	674	0.87
1876	738	656	0.89
1877	698	662	0.95
1878	688	684	0.99½
1879 Jan. 1	686	686	1.00

CHAPTER XVII.

RESUMPTION.

The panic of September, 1873, called attention to the defects of our monetary system. United States notes were hoarded with such avidity that they rose in value to about ninety-three cents in gold or about the value of fractional silver coins — these coins being intentionally debased about seven per cent below their face value to keep them in circulation. President Grant noted this favorable change, and in a letter to Mr. Cowdrey, of October 6, 1873, expressed surprise that silver was not already coming into the market to supply the deficiency in the circulating medium. On the 27th of that month Secretary Richardson issued a circular letter to the several sub-treasury officers, directing them to pay out silver coin to public creditors, should they desire it, in sums not to exceed five dollars in any one payment. At that time the government held of such coin a little less than $450,000, and the step taken by the Secretary, although well intended, brought nothing but ridicule upon the administration. The instructions looking to the paying out of silver coin in this manner were quietly revoked by verbal orders and by private letters.

Upon the assembling of Congress Senator Sherman promptly introduced a measure looking to the resumption of specie payments in gold on January 1, 1876, but it was amended into the inflation measure which was vetoed by the President, to which reference has been made in another chapter; and no further legislation with a view to resumption was attempted during that session. But the action of the President fixed the policy of the Republican party. No steps backward could now be taken. In the next session (December, 1874,) efforts to secure harmonious party action in the future were diligently made. A congressional caucus took upon itself the duties of the finance committee of the Senate and perfected a bill which pleased nobody, but which was the best that could be framed with any prospect of securing its enactment into a law. Mr. Sherman reported the bill to the Senate and, alone, urged its passage. The party whip had done its work and the bill immediately passed, no Republican voting against it except Mr. Schurz. This senator insisted that positive provision should be made in the bill for the retirement of the notes after redemption, a provision which had been necessarily omitted to secure for the support of the bill Mr. Morton and others who had little faith in any scheme for resumption at so early a period.

In the House the bill passed without debate, and the President added his approval January 14, 1875. The act provided (1st) for the redemption of the fractional notes in subsidiary silver coin; (2d) for an unlimited issue of national bank notes with a provision for the retirement of legal tender notes to the extent of eighty per cent of such issue of bank notes until the amount of United States notes outstanding should be reduced to $300,000,000; and (3d) for the redemption in coin of the legal tender notes, on presentation in sums of fifty dollars and upwards at the Sub-Treasury in New York, on and after January 1, 1879. To carry out the provisions of this act, ample authority was given the Secretary of the Treasury to use all surplus revenues of the government, and also to issue such an amount of bonds bearing five, four and a half, or four per cent interest, as he might deem proper. The immediate effect of the passage of the bill was a decrease in the volume of United States notes, as also of national bank notes.

The fractional notes were at that time about at par with fractional silver coin. Silver bullion was therefore purchased, and the mints began the manufacture of fractional coins with which to redeem the fractional notes as provided by law. The Secretary, however, had some doubts as to his authority to pay out the coin in the redemption of the notes, and an act was approved April 17, 1876, directing the exchange to be made and the notes to be permanently retired.

For a time the notes were presented in amounts beyond the capacity of the mints to supply the coins for their redemption, notwithstanding the fact that they were operated over hours and to their maximum capacity.

The amount of fractional notes outstanding was about $42,000,000, but long before that amount was redeemed their presentation for redemption practically ceased. A great demand for the coins continuing, however, Congress authorized the issue of an additional $10,000,000 in exchange for United States notes, these notes to be held as a special deposit with which to redeem the fractional notes when they should be presented for redemption. Straggling fractional notes subsequently reached the Treasury, to some extent, but Congress, convinced that a large amount of them would never be presented for redemption, authorized the United States notes held to be paid out for other purposes. About $15,000,000 of fractional notes still remain outstanding, to that extent constituting a clear gain to the government.

To reimburse the Treasury in part for the money paid out in the purchase of silver bullion, and to make good the deficit occasioned by the retirement of United States notes, Secretary Bristow sold of United States five per cent bonds $17,594,150. The balance needed for these purposes was made up from the surplus revenues. Neither Mr. Bristow nor his successor, Mr. Morrill, took any steps toward accumulating a fund with which to redeem United States notes on Jan. 1, 1879, as provided in the Resumption Act. In March, 1877, Mr. Sherman succeeded Mr. Morrill as Secretary of the Treasury. Of the action taken by this officer the writer has heretofore published the following : —

"On April 6, 1877, Secretary Sherman addressed a letter to a prominent banking firm, in which he announced his purpose to sell bonds to secure coin with which to meet the redemptions required, provided the surplus revenues proved insufficient to enable him to redeem the notes as required by law. He also announced that whenever the sales of four and a half per cent bonds (funded loan of 1891) then being made for refunding purposes reached $200,000,000, he proposed to withdraw from the market the remaining $100,000,000 authorized to be issued for refunding purposes, and to issue thereafter only four per cents (funded loan of 1907). Before the 1st of July ensuing the limit of $200,000,000 was reached, and of the amount sold $15,000,000 were applied to resumption purposes. On the 9th of June a contract was made by the Secretary for the sale of said four per cent bonds, under which also $25,000,000 were reserved for resumption purposes.

"This amount of $40,000,000 was received in gold coin before October, 1877. In that month Congress convened in special session. Among its first measures was the introduction on one day of thirteen bills for the repeal of the Resumption Act. One of these bills passed the House on the 23d of the following month. This extraordinary change of sentiment had been brought about by various causes. The depression in business, which had existed since 1873, was attributed by many to the effects of the Resumption Act.

. . . . .

"During the winter of 1877–78 no further action was taken by the executive officers of the government concerning resumption. On April 1, 1878, in an interview with the House Committee on Banking and Currency, Secretary Sherman announced his purpose to increase the coin reserve by the sale of bonds to the amount of $50,000,000. With this additional amount the total coin reserve in the Treasury applicable to resumption would be about forty per cent of the amount of legal tender notes outstanding; and with this reserve the Secretary thought it would be practicable and prudent to commence the redemption of the notes on the appointed day as required by law.

Four days later negotiations were begun in New York between the Treasury Department and the banks for the sale of four and a half per cent bonds (funded loan of 1891) for this purpose; and after a little delay a sale was effected to the amount of $50,000,000 at a premium of one and a half per cent. The ability of the contracting parties to place the coin in the Treasury as proposed could not be doubted, and from that date there was but little fear of the success of resumption. Further efforts to repeal the law were abandoned, and the business of the country began to adjust itself to the basis of the approaching resumption of specie payments. The payments for the $50,000,000 of bonds were promptly met, and in addition thereto the Treasury reserved of the proceeds of sales of four per cent bonds (funded loan of 1907), then being made, an additional amount of $5,500,000 in gold coin necessary for the extraordinary payment of that amount on account of the so-called "Halifax award."

"In addition to providing the necessary coin reserve, every step was taken by the Treasury which the law would permit to maintain the reserve intact. On the 1st of January, 1879, about $25,000,000 of interest on the public debt, payable in coin, was to fall due; and, as the law required the redemption-reserve fund to be kept in New York, Secretary Sherman determined that the payment of coin on account of interest should thereafter be made only in that city, but gave permission to other Sub-Treasury officers to pay interest to all persons who might be willing to accept legal tender notes. Arrangements were also made with the several assay offices by which gold could be purchased for legal tender notes, whereby the Treasury was replenished to that extent for the probable coin payments in redemption of notes. Steps were also taken by which the government, to a certain extent and for certain purposes, became a member of the Clearing-House Association of New York. Under this arrangement, in consideration of the government's receiving and collecting its checks through the Clearing-House, that body agreed to receive all balances due it upon such checks at the counter of the Sub-Treasury in that city, and to accept legal tender notes in payment of government checks and drafts of all descriptions. As all interest-checks, as well as checks issued in payment of called bonds, were, by law, payable in coin, this agreement on the part of the Clearing-House, through which institution nearly all of the checks passed, relieved the Treasury almost entirely from the necessity of making actual coin payments after resumption took place. This necessity being removed, there was no longer any reason for requiring duties on imports to be paid in coin as provided by law; and the Secretary of the Treasury, in his annual report of December 2, 1878, announced to Congress his purpose to receive notes in payment of such duties. Congress adjourned for the holidays without expressing any opinion as to the legality or advisability of the action proposed, whereupon instructions were given to the government officers to receive such notes in payment of duties, the notes to be redeemed in coin at New York on government account whenever it became necessary. Instructions were also given to the Treasurer and other officers of the Department to close up in their accounts all distinctions between coin and currency, and after January 1, 1879, to recognize, in the accounts as well as in the money, that the government had resumed specie payments, and that the several kinds of money in circulation were of equal value.

"The preparations were so complete that on Jan. 1, 1879, the date when resumption took effect, the Treasurer held, of gold coin and bullion, $135,382,-639.42; of standard silver dollars coined under the act of February 28, 1878, $16,704,829; and of fractional silver coin, including silver bullion, $15,471,265.27. The amount of coin held by the Treasury as available for resumption purposes on that day, after deducting all matured coin liabilities, was about $135,000,000, or about forty per cent of the amount of notes to be redeemed. The thoroughness of preparation for resumption had quieted all apprehensions as to the success of the policy, and on the first day of resumption only straggling demands for coin were made, the amount aggregating less than the amount of notes preferred by the holders of coin obligations. And during the entire year there were redeemed of the legal tender notes only the amount of $11,456,536; while for the same period there were paid out of such notes on account of coin obligations more than $250,000,000. There were also received of such notes in payment of customs dues in the year ending Dec. 31, 1879, $109,467,456.

"Thus, after much labor and sacrifice, the country was lifted out of the financial bog of depreciated paper currency, and with the resumption thus happily secured came a revival of business, an extraordinary demand for labor of all kinds, and a confirmation of that confidence which was so necessary for all business enterprises, and which had grown step by step with every movement made toward a specie basis."

The whole amount of the reserve is carried as a part of the ordinary Treasury balance, subject to the warrant of the Secretary at any time and perhaps for any purpose. The Secretary, in his annual report for 1879, called the attention of Congress to the matter, and recommended that to avoid all uncertainty this fund be specifically defined and set apart for the redemption of United

States notes, and that the notes redeemed be reissued only in exchange for or purchase of coin or bullion.

Congress, by an act approved July 12, 1882, provided that the issue of gold certificates should be suspended whenever the amount of gold reserved in the Treasury for the redemption of United States notes should fall below $100,000,000, thus indirectly recognizing that amount as constituting the reserve fund.

In an act approved July 12, 1890, authorizing Treasury notes in payment of silver bullion, which notes were made redeemable in gold or silver coin at the discretion of the Secretary of the Treasury, Congress declared it to be "the established policy of the United States to maintain the two metals on a parity with each other upon the present legal ratio, or such ratios as may be provided by law."

Under the authority of this act the Secretary has, in order to maintain the parity, redeemed not only the notes in question, but silver certificates and United States notes in gold or silver as the holder demanded, using therefor any specie in the Treasury, reimbursing the account as he deemed proper by the sale of bonds for coin under the authority of the Resumption Act and section 3700 of the Revised Statutes, the latter being the reproduction of section 1, act March 17, 1862, as follows:

"The Secretary of the Treasury may purchase coin with any of the bonds or notes of the United States authorized by law, at such rates and upon such terms as he may deem most advantageous to the public interest."

Doubtless the failure of the revenue laws to provide a sufficient revenue greatly influenced the presentation of notes for redemption and led to the impingement upon the reserve. But at best through unwise legislation the amount of notes redeemable from the fund has been so greatly increased as to temporarily impair the soundness of the paper currency, and the business of the country is again suffering through the interference of politics in the monetary circulation.

CHAPTER XVIII.

THE SUPREME COURT.

The act of Congress authorizing the issue of legal tender notes was a partisan measure, no Democrat voting for it. The act providing for the redemption of the notes in coin was framed in a Republican caucus, and carried through both Houses by force of party discipline. The courts of fifteen of the States have affirmed, from time to time, the constitutional power of Congress to issue such notes, the judges dividing in their opinion on the subject according to their political affinities; and the court of only one State has denied to Congress this power, — the Court of Appeals of the State of Kentucky. In this court the opinion was unanimous, but the judges were not of opposing politics. In the Supreme Court of the United States the justices have divided upon the subject whenever it has been brought before them, according to party prejudice. The action of this court on the legal tender question constitutes one of the most remarkable chapters in the history of that tribunal. The first decision pertaining thereto arose in the now celebrated case of Hepburn *v.* Griswold. The facts in this case are briefly as follows:—

A certain Mrs. Hepburn of Kentucky, on the 20th of June, 1860, made a promissory note to one Henry Griswold, by the terms of which she was to pay to the order of said Griswold $11,250, on the 20th of February, 1862. At the time of the making and maturity of the note there was not in the United States any legal tender money except gold and silver coin. The note, however, was not paid at maturity, and interest therefore accumulated upon it. On the 25th day of February, 1862, Congress passed the act authorizing the issue of United States notes, and making them a legal tender in the payment of private debts. In March, 1864, the Hepburn note not having been paid, suit was brought upon it, and the maker tendered in payment $12,770 in United States notes, that being the undisputed amount of note and interest. This tender was refused on the ground that it changed the terms of the contract, coin being the only legal tender money when the note was made. The Chancellor of the Court, however, declared the tender good, and adjudicated the claim to be settled accordingly. The payee, however, was not satisfied and appealed the matter to the Court of Errors, where the Chancellor's judgment was reversed. The maker of the note was now dissatisfied, and she carried the case to the Supreme Court of the United States. In that court the case was first argued during the December term, 1867, and it was elaborately reargued in the December term, 1868, especially with reference to the constitutional power of Congress to authorize the issue of such legal tender notes. The case was withheld for decision until the December term, 1869, when, by a majority of the court, the act was declared to be unconstitutional, so far as it made the notes a legal tender for debts existing prior to the date of the authorizing act of Feb. 25, 1862. When this decision was made the court consisted of eight justices, there being one vacancy. The five justices concurring in the opinion were Chief Justice Chase, and Associate Justices Nelson, Clifford, Field, and Greer. Justice Miller read the dissenting opinion, in which Justices Swayne and Davis concurred. The court divided in accordance with the political sympathies of the justices composing it. It may be alleged that the Chief Justice was known as a prominent member of the Republican party, but it will be remembered that for some time his sympathies with that party had somewhat abated, and while the case in question was pending before the court, he had been a prominent candidate for presidential honors at the hands of the Democratic party.

The judgment of the court was generally approved, but there was a considerable feeling that in some way the "greenbacks" had helped the country through the war, and that a like necessity for help might again arise, and for the country to deprive itself of any power likely to be needed in such an emergency would be political suicide. Hence arose a demand that the opinion of the court should be reversed. The case decided could not, however, under a rule of the court, be reargued, except upon the request of one of the judges who had joined in affirming the decision, and none of them asked to have the case reopened.

Mr. Justice Greer, however, resigned,— his resignation to take effect Feb. 1, 1870; and Mr. Strong took his place as justice on the 14th of March following. Mr. Bradley took his seat as an additional justice ten days later. It has been alleged, and never denied, that one or both of these gentlemen had formerly been employed as counsel for the Camden and Amboy Railroad, and, as such counsel, had given opinions affirming the legal tender act to be constitutional; and also that both held considerable stock of that corporation. It was known, too, that, subsequent to the decision in the Hepburn case, the company, in paying interest on its obligations contracted previous to 1862, had, in accordance with the opinion of their counsel, made a reservation looking to the reversal of judgment in that case, by which reversal the indebtedness of the road could be paid in United States notes instead of coin.[1]

The opinions of these two gentlemen on the power to issue legal tender notes were therefore well known, and the proceedings of the court immediately following their entering upon official duty has given color to the oft-repeated assertions that the court was organized to secure a reversal of the legal tender decision. The next day after Justice Bradley took his seat, Friday, the 26th of March, the Attorney General moved the court that certain cases appealed from the Court of Claims should be set down for argument, and suggested that the legal tender decision might be reconsidered in these cases. The next day the motion was considered, and, contrary to the wishes of the justices who had joined in the opinion in the Hepburn case, an order was directed that the cases in question should be heard on the 4th day of April following, being the second Monday next ensuing. This order was in disregard of the usual practice of the court, the time for argument in such cases being usually fixed by counsel subject to the approval of the court. Before the order was announced, however, Mr. Carlisle, the attorney for the appellants, protested against a re-argument of the legal-tender question in these cases, the rights of his clients, he asserted, having been already determined. The

Schuckers' Life of Chase.

court, therefore, on Monday morning deferred the announcement of the order for the re-argument of the cases until the protest of Mr. Carlisle could be considered, and the time for considering the protest was fixed for the next day (Tuesday) after adjournment of the court, and this happened accordingly.

After hearing Mr. Carlisle the court immediately ordered that the matters involved in the motion of the Attorney General should be argued on the Thursday following; that the subject should be considered in conference immediately after the adjournment of the court for that day; and that the result should be announced on the opening of the court the following morning. This order was made against the remonstrances of the justices who had agreed in the judgment of the Hepburn case, and it is alleged that so far as the history of the court is known the order was unprecedented. The regular motion day of the court was Friday, the regular conference day Saturday, and in no recorded case had there been any anticipation of the regular order of business for those days in order to reach a special case.

The order was, however, carried into effect, an argument in progress being suspended that the cases might be heard. That in itself constituted another unprecedented movement. The conference was held after adjournment, and a new order was passed, regardless of the convenience of counsel, directing that the cases be heard in all matters involved in the records on the 11th of the following month, but the time was subsequently extended to the 18th.

These cases had previously been continued under the order of the court, distinctly stated by the Chief Justice, and acquiesced in by the counsel, by the appellants, and by the government, that the legal tender question should not be reopened, but that both sides should abide by the decision in the Hepburn case. The Chief Justice called the attention of the justices to these facts, but without effect. The appellants in these cases, however, knowing well enough what would be the decision of the court, decided to withdraw the cases, and so, when the time for argument arrived, their counsel moved that the cases be dismissed. To this motion the Attorney General and Justices Miller and Bradley objected, but, after consultation, the court granted the motion, Justice Bradley objecting. The opportunity to reverse the decision in the Hepburn case was lost at present, but the country knew that the reversal would come in due time, and the fact of such reversal was discounted. The appointment of these two justices, whose opinion on the legal tender question was well known in advance, the fact of their connection with a great railroad corporation, and their well-known ownership of its stock, the haste of the court in attempting to secure a reversal of the legal tender decision together, created a painful impression that other interests than those of the government were being served.

The court had not long to wait for an opportunity to reverse the opinion, as had been foreshadowed in the December term, 1870. Several cases came up similar in character, the controlling questions of which were:—

1st. Are the acts of Congress known as the legal tender acts constitutional when applied to contracts made before their passage?

2d. Are they valid as applicable to debts contracted since their enactment?

The cases were considered in the full bench, and by a vote of five to four the court held such acts of Congress constitutional as applied to contracts made either before or after the passage of the acts, thus overruling the previous decision in the matter. The opinion was rendered by Mr. Justice Strong, and concurred in by Justices Bradley, Miller, Davis, and Swayne; Chief Justice Chase delivered a dissenting opinion, as did also Justices Nelson, Clifford, and Field, the court being again divided in accordance with the opposing politics of the justices composing it.

In delivering the opinion of the court, Justice Strong recounted the exigencies of the government which brought the notes into existence, and maintained that Congress, in such an emergency, being called upon to devise means for maintaining the army and navy,—in fact to preserve the government created by the Constitution,—not only had the power to issue the notes, but that the condition of affairs justified such an issue. He also plainly intimated that Congress, under its constitutional power to coin money and to regulate the value thereof, could at any time declare Treasury notes a legal tender, if such declaration should be adapted to carrying into execution the admitted powers of the government.

The power of Congress to issue Treasury notes at any time and in any amount, and to make them a legal tender in payment of private debts, has since been distinctly affirmed by the court.

The act of May 31, 1878, prohibited the further retirement of United States notes, and provided that when any of the notes might be redeemed or paid into the Treasury, they should not be retired or cancelled, but should be reissued and paid out again and kept in circulation. The effect of this act, so far as it applied to the reissue of notes that had been redeemed, was to authorize the issue of new legal tender notes in time of peace, and when no necessity of the government required such an emission. A case testing the power of Congress to thus authorize the issue of such notes was carried to the Supreme Court on a writ of error, and a decision therein was rendered by the court in March, 1884. A synopsis of the decision prepared by the court is as follows: —

"The question presented by this case, as it is stated by the court, is 'whether notes of the United States, issued in time of war, under acts of Congress declaring them to be a legal tender in payment of private debts, and afterward, in time of peace, redeemed and paid in gold coin at the Treasury, and then reissued under the act of 1878, can, under the Constitution of the United States, be a legal tender in payment of such debts.' . . .

"The court holds, therefore, that Congress has the power to issue the obligations of the United States in such form, and to impress upon them such qualities as currency for the purchase of merchandise and the payment of debts as accord with the usage of sovereign governments. The power, as incident to the power of borrowing money and issuing bills and notes of the government for money borrowed, of impressing upon those bills or notes the quality of being a legal tender for the payment of private debts, was a power universally understood to belong to sovereignty in Europe and America at the time of the framing and adoption of the Constitution of the United States.

"This power of making the notes of the United Sates a legal tender in payment of private debts, being included in the power to borrow money and to provide a national currency, is not defeated nor restricted by the fact that its exercise may affect the value of private contracts. If, upon a just and fair interpretation of the whole Constitution, a particular power or authority appears to be vested in Congress, it is no constitutional objection to its existence or to its exercise, that the property or the contracts of individuals may be incidentally affected.

"Congress," the court says, in conclusion, "as the legislature of a sovereign nation, being expressly empowered by the Constitution 'to lay and collect taxes to pay the debts and provide for the common defence and general welfare of the United States,' and 'to borrow money on the credit of the United States,' and 'to coin money and regulate the value thereof and of foreign coin," and being clearly authorized, as incidental to the exercise of those great powers, to emit bills of credit, to charter national banks, and to provide a national currency for the whole people, in the form of coin, Treasury notes, and national bank bills, and the power to make the notes of the government a legal tender in payment of private debts being one of the powers belonging to sovereignty in other civilized nations, and not expressly withheld from Congress by the Constitution, we are irresistibly impelled to the conclusion that the impressing upon the Treasury notes of the United States the quality of being a legal tender in the payment of private debts is an appropriate means, conducive and plainly adapted to the execution of the undoubted powers of Congress, consistent with the letter and spirit of the Constitution, and therefore, within the meaning of that instrument, 'necessary and proper for carrying into execution the powers vested by this Constitution in the government of the United States.'

"Such being our conclusion in the matter of law, the question whether at any particular time, in war or in peace, the exigency is such, by reason of unusual and pressing demands on the resources of the government, or of the inadequacy of the supply of gold and silver coin to furnish the currency needed for the uses of the government and of the people, that it is, as a matter of fact, wise and expedient to resort to this means, is a political question, to be determined by Congress when the question of exigency arises, and not a judicial question to be afterward passed upon by the courts.

"It follows that the act of May 31, 1878, is constitutional and valid, and that the circuit court rightly held that the tender in Treasury notes reissued and kept in circulation under that act was a tender of lawful money in payment of the defendant's debt to the plaintiff.

"The judgment of the Circuit Court is affirmed." Opinion by Justice Gray. Justice Field dissenting.

In this decision a political line is again drawn among the justices, but prominent men of both parties are already alarmed at the dangerous doctrine enunciated by the court.

Article 10 of the amendments to the Constitution is as follows: —

"The powers not delegated to the United States by the Constitution, nor prohibited by it to the States, are reserved to the States respectively, or to the people."

The court holds that in the issue of notes Congress has such power as accords " with the usage of sovereign governments," and that the power " of impressing upon these bills or notes the quality of being a legal tender in the payment of private debts was a power universally understood to belong to sovereignty in Europe and America at the time of the framing and adoption of the Constitution of the United States."

No such omnipotent power was ever claimed for Congress by the most ultra federalist in the early days of the Republic, as that conceded to it by this court, and measures looking to a reversal of the decision of the court by an amendment to the Constitution expressly prohibiting to Congress such powers have already been introduced into that body. Such an amendment will, in time, doubtless become a part of the organic law of the land. Meanwhile the sacredness of contracts, the stability of wealth, the success of business enterprises, and the prosperity of the whole country, must depend upon the integrity of that body, whose actions have too often been the result of successful log-rolling, or been dictated by a political caucus.

Thirty years ago this same court decided that the negro had no rights which the white man was bound to respect, and only four years of bloody war reversed the decision. An amendment to the Constitution, reversing the legal tender decision of the same court, should be vigorously pressed to adoption in season to prevent, not another war, but national disgrace and bankruptcy.

CHAPTER XIX:

GOLD COIN AND CERTIFICATES.

The coinage act of April 2, 1792, which embodied the recommendations of Mr. Hamilton, provided for the manufacture of certain gold coins, as follows: Eagles, each to be of the value of ten units or dollars, and to contain $247\frac{1}{2}$ grains of pure gold, or 270 grains of standard, thus making these coins eleven-twelfths fine; and half-eagles and quarter-eagles, of the same fineness and of proportional weight. The act also provided for the coinage of silver dollars or units, each to be of the value of the Spanish milled dollar, containing $371\frac{1}{4}$ grains of pure silver, or 416 grains of standard silver; and of halves, quarters, and dimes or tenths, of the same fineness and proportionate weight. Coinage of both gold and silver coin was to be free to all persons bringing bullion to the mint for that purpose. All the coins were to be legal tender in all payments for their face value.

The legal relation in weight of pure gold to pure silver was thus fixed by this act at 1 to 15.

This ratio happened to be nearly the commercial one for the year 1793; but it was too small for the next year, and too large for the two succeeding years. In 1797 the commercial ratio was 1 to 15.45; in 1799 it was 1 to 14.29; in 1809 it was 1 to 16.25; and up to the present time, in one year only (1813), has it ever been less than 1 to 15. Gold was therefore, on the whole, undervalued, and consequently little of it came to be coined, and less went into circulation. Silver coins were still manufactured at the mints, but bank issues and foreign coins furnished most of the circulating medium of the country. The bank issues were, however, uncertain in value, and in some parts of the country a considerable demand arose for a coin circulation, whereupon the question of a circulating medium at once got into politics. The Democratic party, headed by Senator Benton, of Missouri, demanded that the weight of gold coin should be so reduced as to equalize its commercial value to a corresponding amount of silver coin; or, if there was to be any difference, that gold should be so underrated as to ensure its circulation. Mr. Benton asserted that, in adjusting at any time the relative value of gold and silver so as to retain both in circulation, there was a nicety, but no difficulty. Such adjustment, he asserted, was the proper work for a committee of Congress. Several nations of antiquity had accomplished it, some modern nations also, among which were England and France; and he intimated that in the latter country the adjustment was established by the genius of Napoleon.

As England had adopted the single standard of gold in 1816, and as gold then circulated in France only at a premium in silver, his mention of the modern nations which had achieved the simultaneous circulation of both metals was not so happy as to create any curiosity as to which were the nations of antiquity to which he referred.

But relief from the alleged evils of Hamilton's coinage act was at hand. A measure was introduced into Congress before which, Mr. Benton said, the machinery of distress was to balk. The bill originated in the House, and provided for "equalizing the value of gold and silver," and "legalizing the foreign coins of both metals." The ratio between the two metals was fixed at 1 to 15⅝. Mr. Benton, in his "Thirty Years' View," states that this ratio at first commended itself to all who seemed best calculated, from their pursuits, to understand the subject; that the majority of speakers, and the eighteen banks of New York, with Mr. Gallatin at their head, favored it; that the difficulty of adjusting this ratio so that neither metal could expel the other had been a stumbling-block for a great many years; and now this difficulty seemed to be as formidable as ever; that refined calculations were gone into, scientific light was sought, history was rummaged back to the times of the Roman empire; but that there seemed to be no way to get an accord of opinion, either from the lights of science, the voice of history, or the results of calculation.

About this time, however, a political breeze sprung up which helped the friends of gold out of their troubled waters. There was a determined effort on the part of the administration to get rid of the National Bank and its issues; and to popularize that movement the introduction of gold to take the place of the notes in circulation was advocated, and the scheme met with much favor. The celebrated author of the "View" suddenly found that the ratio of 1 to 16 was the true one for the coinage of the metals. It would be a reflection upon his intelligence to presume that he did not know that under the operations of that ratio, whatever might become of the notes, silver would be underrated and would leave the country as gold had done under the ratio of 1 to 15. There was, however, so little of our silver in circulation that the matter of its retention or expulsion was of no especial moment. The subject will be more fully discussed under the heading of Silver Dollars and Certificates.

The proposed measure became a law June 28, 1834. Under this act the eagle was to contain

232 grains of pure gold, or 258 grains of standard gold, a reduction in weight of 15½ grains of pure gold. The half-eagle and quarter-eagle were to be of equal fineness and proportionate weight.*

Upon the passage of this act Mr. Benton and his friends were in high glee, but their joy was brief. The gold coins were so reduced in weight that it was now cheaper to pay debts in them than in silver coin. In consequence no more silver was coined for circulation, and the amount then in circulation at once disappeared, being sent abroad in payment of obligations, or melted down for other uses at home. This sudden contraction of the currency created considerable distress, and the loss of the small silver pieces caused no little inconvenience. The panic of 1837 followed. Depreciated bank bills, " shin plasters," and a few worn Mexican pieces came into circulation to take the place of full-weight silver pieces, which had been superseded by the cheaper gold coins. The author of the " View " admits that he was now called a " Gold Humbug; " that the newspapers expended their wit " in stale depreciation of his efforts; " but while apparently unable to explain what had become of the silver which the experience of Mexico led him to suppose would circulate with gold, he still vaunted the excellence of his scheme, boasted of a coming abundance of his favorite metal, and

* In 1837 the amount of pure gold in these coins was slightly reduced to make the standard nine-tenths fine, and the ratio 1 to 15.98, commonly known, however, as 1 to 16.

prophesied that at some day "gold would flow up the Mississippi and spread through the land." Gold did come, all that was wanted, but with it came no benefits sufficient to compensate for the disappearance of silver.

By the reduction in the weight of the gold coins the gold dollar became the unit of account, changing the terms of all pre-existing contracts payable in dollars to the extent of its depreciation below the value of the silver dollar.

It remained the unit of value until, by the act of February 25, 1862, the paper issues of the government thereby authorized were declared a legal tender in payment of debt. Gold now became a commodity, and was quoted at a premium, as was silver when gold took its place. Duties on imports and interest on public debt were, however, still payable by law in coin, and enough gold coin to meet these payments remained in circulation. To avoid handling the actual coin, the fifth section of an act approved March 3, 1863, authorized the Secretary of the Treasury to receive gold coin or bullion on deposit, and to issue therefor certificates in denominations of not less than $20, to be used in payment of coin interest, and to be receivable in payment of customs dues. The coin deposited was to be held for the redemption of the certificates. The issue of these certificates proved to be a great convenience to brokers, bankers, and bullion dealers, who in this way had use of the Treasury vaults in which to store specie free of risk and expense to themselves.

Although the issue of United States notes drove most of the gold from circulation, foreign exchanges continued to be made in terms of that metal; hence commerce was compelled to recognize two kinds of money, although but one was in general circulation. This condition of affairs brought into existence the Gold Board of New York, at which exchanges of gold and currency could be made, and the rates of exchange prevailing at this Board fixed throughout the country the relation between the two. As long as the government retained the luxury of two kinds of money, the existence of this Board was a convenience, if not a necessity, to persons engaged in foreign trade. Its operations may be thus illustrated: A Liverpool cotton merchant telegraphs to the New York commission house, "If you can buy one thousand bales of middling cotton so as not to cost me more than ten pence or twenty cents gold per pound, laid down in Liverpool, you may do so." The commission merchant finds that the freight, insurance, and other charges will amount to about two cents. He can therefore afford to give eighteen cents, gold, for the cotton itself. He goes into the cotton market and inquires the price of cotton in gold. The dealer answers that cotton is sold for notes, not for gold; that the planters in the South pay their laborers and buy their provisions and agricultural implements with notes; and that they can tell what their cotton costs them in notes, but not what it is worth in gold. The price of cotton is 27 cents a pound in notes. His next inquiry is to ascertain the price of gold, so as to know how much in notes he can afford to pay for the cotton without exceeding the orders of his Liverpool correspondent. He finds gold selling at 150. In other words, his 18 cents gold are worth exactly 27 cents in notes, and he can therefore buy his cotton at this rate without exceeding his correspondent's orders. Thus far the transaction is simple enough. He has only to take as much gold as would pay for the thousand bales of cotton, sell it at 150, and with the notes pay the cotton dealer, and the whole transaction is concluded. But the Liverpool merchant has not sent the gold. It will be several days before the cotton will be ready for shipment, and not until thus ready will payment for it be made. Should he contract for the cotton without any assurance at what rate he could dispose of his gold when received, he would take a risk of loss in case the value of gold should in the meanwhile depreciate. To avoid this risk he contracts at the Gold Board to sell sufficient gold to pay for the cotton at 150, the gold to be delivered at his option, within say ten days. He now can purchase his cotton with safety, store it aboard the vessel, and procure the bill of lading therefor. This bill of lading he presents to a dealer in foreign exchange, obtains the gold therefor, which he delivers to the party to whom he has previously sold it, and the transaction is closed. Without the intervention of the Gold Board he would have run the risk of paying more for his cotton than his correspondent had authorized.

What was a useful and necessary adjunct to transactions involving exchanges with foreign countries became a resort for fictitious trading, and fortunes there changed hands as rapidly as they ever did on the green cloth of Baden or Monaco. Nor was the speculation confined to New York. Telegraphic indicators furnished to all the cities quotations of the ever-changing price of gold. Speculation was raised to a feverish height throughout the country, and attention was turned to the Gold Board in New York as eagerly as to the embattled army at the front, engaged in a life-and-death struggle for the nation. The fluctuations in the price of gold in 1863 and 1864 were remarkable. Gold was quoted on the 1st of January, 1863, at 134; on the 24th at 150; on the 31st at 160; on the 12th of February at $154\frac{1}{2}$, and on the 28th at 172¼. The price then began to decline, and on the 28th of March gold stood at 143⅛; on the 28th of August at 122¼, and the lowest figure for 1863; but the fluctuations continued during the remainder of the year, resulting, on the whole, in a considerable advance in the price. On the 1st of January, 1864, gold was quoted at 152; on the 26th of February at 169½; on April 12th it was 175; and on the 26th it ran up to 184; on the 10th of May it was 168; and on the 27th 186¼. These fluctuations reacted upon prices, and turned the most legitimate of business enterprises into a kind of gambling. The government had brought about this condition of affairs by its unfortunate legislation, and to the government everybody turned for relief. As the gold paid into the public Treasury on account of duties on imports was in excess of its requirements for the payment of interest, the government owned a considerable amount of that coin. It was now generally supposed that if the government should enter the market as a "bear," the premium on gold would be reduced. Accordingly Congress, in March, 1864, authorized the Secretary of the Treasury to dispose of any surplus gold in the Treasury by selling it for other currency.

On the 12th of April following the passage of this act, gold reached 175, and seemed likely to reach a far higher figure. Secretary Chase was urged from all quarters to enter the market, sell cash gold, break down the premium, and teach the gold gamblers a lesson. To these entreaties he yielded, and on the evening of April 13 he started for New York, at which city he arrived the next morning. The "bulls," notwithstanding the august presence of so important an official, showed fight, and during the day tossed the premium to 89. The Secretary was, however, armed with the authority of Congress, a body to which had been delegated the power to regulate money, and he opened wide the vaults of the Sub-Treasury, and poured into Wall Street $11,000,000 of solid gold, striking a momentary terror to the hearts of his adversaries. But the next day he wrote to the President: "The sales which have been made here yesterday and to-day seem to reduce the price, but the reduction is only temporary." The Secretary returned to the Department, and as soon as the pressure was removed the premium rapidly advanced, and gold, on the 20th of April, was quoted at 184.

The result of the governmental bearing operations in Wall Street was, one would think, sufficiently convincing that even the great power of Congress was unequal to the task of controlling the market. But Congress admitted no such incapacity. There was yet one untried resource, the majesty of a restraining law. A bill was promptly introduced in the Senate, the purpose of which was, as stated by Senator Sherman, to prevent gambling in gold. It prevented sales of coin for future deliveries, and it prohibited also any sale of gold by any broker or banker at other than his regular place of business. The penalty for the violation of this act was to be a fine of not less than $1,000, nor more than $10,000, and imprisonment not less than three months nor more than one year, or both, at the discretion of the Court. Mr. Shuckers, the biographer of Secretary Chase, says this bill was the result of a protracted consultation between the Secretary, experienced financial gentlemen, and members of Congress, who agreed generally that if the bill did no good, it was not likely to do much harm. This acknowledgment of doubt was creditable to the intelligence of the gentlemen in conference, but it must have been humiliating to the pride of the Congressional portion; for had not the Constitution declared that Congress had power to regulate the value of money, and had not the author of the legal tender act declared that, by the success of that measure, the government would avoid "shinning" through Wall Street?

The bill for the suppression of gambling in gold became a law June 17, 1864, and went at once into operation. Its disturbing effect upon the price of gold became at once conspicuous

On the 20th gold closed at 198½; on the next day the act was authoritatively notified to the Gold Board, and its evil effects became apparent. Gold ceased to be called at the Board, but no power could prevent men from dealing in it. Gold stood on the 21st at 208; the next day at 230, but closed at 213; on the 27th it reached 238; on the 29th, 250; on the 1st of July it reached 280, then fell to 255, and closed at 225. The next day it fluctuated between 225 and 237. By this time Congress was impressed with the disastrous result of its legislation, and began to talk of repealing this act, which, at worst, its advocates thought, could do no harm. On the 6th the act was repealed, but too late; the mischief had been done. Violent fluctuations followed in the feverish market which the act had created; on the 10th the rate varied between 260 and 270; and the next morning it was 285, the highest point reached during the war. From this point it receded, but slowly. Of course, the stock, grain, and provision markets were strongly affected, and the calamitous effect of the act was felt in the increased price of commodities. Perhaps no greater amount of evil was ever crowded into so brief a period by the interference of legislation with the functions of a circulating medium; certainly no measure more disastrous and humiliating has ever been transferred from a political conference to the statutes of this country.

Congress made no further attempt to control the gold market, but as coin accumulated in the Treasury beyond need for coin payments, the Secretary was compelled, from time to time, to sell the surplus for notes which were needed in current transactions. These sales necessarily affected the markets more or less, but this disturbance could not be avoided as long as depreciated paper furnished the circulating medium.

The Treasury also tried other schemes to repress the advance in the gold premium. For a time it privately sold exchanges on London through the National Bank of Commerce in New York, and also publicly through the New York Sub-Treasury. It also issued to importers gold certificates of deposit upon the deposit of United States notes, at one-quarter of one per cent less than the current rate of coin. These certificates were not negotiable, and were receivable in payment of customs dues at their face value; but, despite every precaution, they became subject to speculation, and this plan, for which a great triumph in checking gold speculation was predicted, was found to be so inconvenient and dangerous that, after a few weeks, it was abandoned.

For a time the sale of gold was conducted privately through the Sub-Treasury in New York, but, after 1867, contemplated sales were usually announced several days in advance, and generally were limited in amount to the needs of the public service.

Chief among the schemes of speculators during these occurrences was that of making gold scarce in order to "move the crops." It was plausibly urged by them that farmers would withhold grain from the market until a certain price therefor in paper could be obtained. As the gold premium advanced, prices advanced, consequently the point at which wheat would be sold could be reached by making gold scarce and the premium high. To the exporter of grain the increase of premium was of no moment. He was paid for his shipments in coin, and he could, without loss, increase the price to be paid the purchaser precisely as the premium increased. As prices of other commodities followed the rise in premium, the money the farmer obtained for his wheat, at the higher rate, was worth no more to him than the lower.

This newly found device for moving the crops met with great favor among many public officials, and was diligently advocated by speculators, who, while pretending to be shipping grain, were really speculating in the rise in the gold premium.

In the summer of 1869 gold was quoted at about 135. Sales of gold by the Treasury, in the amount of $1,000,000, were being made every alternate Wednesday. An abundant grain crop had been harvested throughout the west, and shipments of grain to the seaboard were made as freely as prices would warrant; but the speculators made a great outcry that the Treasury should increase the gold premium and further stimulate the movement of the crops. In August, certain well-known gentlemen in New York joined in a gold speculation, operating for an increase in the premium. To secure success they desired,

1st. To know precisely how much gold was held by the banks and the Treasury.

2d. To have the ordinary sales of gold suspended. And —

3d. To be assured that in case of a rise in the premium the Treasury would not interfere by selling gold.

They knew that outside of the Treasury there was comparatively but a small amount of gold, perhaps not $25,000,000 all told. By purchasing gold persistently at the Gold Board, they believed they could obtain control of all the gold in the street, and force the settlement of contracts upon their own terms. A relative of the President was associated with them in the enterprise, and there is reason to believe that the Assistant Treasurer at New York aided the scheme. Of the action taken in this matter by public officials the records show as follows: —

On August 18, the Assistant Treasurer at New York addressed a letter to the Secretary of the Treasury, stating that he was under apprehension with regard to gold certificates issued by his office, and suggesting that the national bank examiners in the principal cities be instructed, on a certain fixed day, to run over the specie items of the banks, and to take a brief record of the amounts held in gold and in certificates. Two days later he recommended that the inquiry be extended to the several Treasury offices.

The information asked for would, if furnished, have been wholly useless to him for any purpose of checking his record of issues, for which he claimed to desire it. A numerical record of every certificate issued was kept at the Treasury as well as at his own office, and the amount outstanding could at any time have been verified with very little labor; but in order to answer his request the Acting Secretary called upon the banks and the Treasurer of the United States to report the respective amounts of gold and of gold certificates held by the banks and in the Treasury on the morning of the 8th day of September following.

Meanwhile the projectors of the scheme had not been idle. They had secured an interview with the President, and impressed him with the importance of moving the crops promptly by suspending the sale of gold until the premium became high enough to induce the farmers to part with their wheat.

On August 30, one of the clique addressed a letter to the Secretary of the Treasury, complimenting him for refraining from putting gold on the market at that season of the year, when the bulk of our agricultural products was to be marketed, and explaining to him the great advantages which would result from a policy which could not but enrich the whole country by causing a large exportation of grain and other agricultural products. On the 20th he wrote again, reasserting his opinion that the premium on gold should be maintained.

"In my judgment," he said, "the government cannot afford to sell gold during the next three months while the crops are being marketed, and if such a policy were announced it would immediately cause a high export of breadstuffs and an active fall trade." This specious reasoning had its effect upon the President, and he addressed a letter about the 3d of September to the Secretary of the Treasury, then away from Washington, in which he expressed the opinion that it was undesirable to force down the price of gold. He spoke of the importance to the West of being able to move its crops. On the 12th he addressed another letter from New York, stating that a desperate struggle was then taking place between the bulls and bears of Wall Street, and that each party wanted the government to help it out. He advised the Secretary to move on without change until the struggle was over. On the 20th the Treasury Department sent to the Assistant Treasurer at New York the information that he desired in reference to the coin and coin certificates held by the national banks.

On the same day the member of the clique who had previously written to the Secretary wrote that there was a panic in Wall Street, engineered by a bear combination, which had withdrawn currency to such an extent that it was impossible to do ordinary business. He now advised that, until the crops were moved, the banks should be given some currency out of the Treasury reserve. The facts were, that the clique of which he was a member, having matured all their plans, had several days before commenced the purchase of gold, running up the price to such an extent that all business was disturbed and an artificial stringency in the currency created. On the morning of the 24th of September, gold was at 150, before noon at 162, and the excitement in Wall Street was unprecedented. At 11.45 that day the Secretary telegraphed the Assistant Treasurer to sell $4,000,000 of gold. This broke the combination, and gold, in fifteen minutes, was selling at 140 for cash For once the Treasury was in Wall Street with effect, either for good or for evil.

Of the allegations that were frequently made, that public officials aided in this plot, there never was a shadow of proof, except, perhaps, in the case of the Assistant Treasurer at New York. For the part he took in the affair he was compelled to resign his position. The result of the combination was immense loss to many innocent individuals, and the wreck of some of the clique to whom the others proved unfaithful. A general disturbance was felt throughout the whole country, and gave to the day in which the scheme culminated the name of "Black Friday," which will be long remembered in the annals of the country. Of the operations of the parties other than government officials, the following account, taken from a newspaper published at that time, furnishes full information: —

"In the spacious exchange room of the Gold Board, crowded as it had never been crowded, even in the wildest excitement of war times, amid the strangest variations of deathlike silence and tumultuous uproar, the pallid, half conscience-stricken brokers of this gambling clique appeared, one after another, to do their dirty work. By the little fountain which plays in the centre of the floor, and around which the principal business is transacted, first one bid arose, 145 for $100,000, and there was no response. Then another bid, 146 for $100,000, and again no answer; 146, 147, 148, 149 for $100,000, with a pause between each, all amid deathlike silence.

"The hundreds gathered there, and the thousands who read the ominous words on all the telegraphic indicators in the principal business offices in the city, and the hundreds of thousands who watched the telegraph offices throughout the country, stood appalled. Each one per cent advance involved losses of millions; the gain was with the clique. Who could tell what would be the end? There was no resisting such power. They could advance to 200 if they chose. And the usually surging, bustling, shouting mass of humanity crowded there was held silent, almost motionless, as by a magic spell. One hundred and fifty is now bid for $100,000, and despair suddenly gives back life to many. They rush eagerly to bid and buy. Orders come in by telegraph to buy at any price. Messengers from all parts of the city, the great bankers, the merchant princes, from up-town and down-town, force their way in through the crush, and give back to the brokers the sense of reality which they seem to have lost amid the dream-like terror. The stillness is suddenly succeeded by frantic excitement. Transactions of enormous magnitude are made amid the wildest confusion, and the most unearthly screaming of men, always excitable, now driven to the verge of temporary insanity by the consciousness of ruin, or the delusive dream of immense wealth. But amid all the noise and confusion the penetrating voices of the leading brokers of the clique are still heard advancing the price at each bid, and increasing the amount of their bids at each advance, until at last, with voice overtopping the bedlam below, the memorable bid burst forth, '160 for any part of $5,000,000.' Again the noise was hushed. Terror became depicted on every countenance. Cool, sober men looked at one another, and noted the ashy paleness that spread over all. Even those who had but little or no interest at stake were seized with the infection of fear, and were conscious of a great evil approaching. And from the silence again came forth that shrieking bid, '160 for $5,000,000,' and no answer; '161 for $5,000,-000,' '162 for $5,000,000,' still no answer; '162 for any part of $5,000,000.' And a quiet voice said, 'Sold $1,000,000 at 162.'

"That quiet voice broke the fascination. The bid of 162 was not renewed. But 161 was again bid for a million, and the same quiet voice said, 'Sold;' and the bid of 161 was not renewed. But 160 was again bid for $5,000,000. Then dimly it dawned upon the quicker-witted ones that, for some reason or other, the game was up. As if by magnetic sympathy the same thought passed through the crowd at once. A dozen men leaped furiously at the bidder, and claimed to have sold the whole $5,000,000. To their horror the bidder stood his ground and declared he would take all.

"But before the words had fairly passed his lips, before the terror at his action had had time to gain men's hearts, there was a rush amid the crowd. New men, wild with fresh excitement, crowded to the barriers. In an instant the rumor was abroad, 'The Treasury is selling.' Quick as thought men realized that it was not safe to sell to the clique brokers. Scarcely any one now wanted to buy. All who had bought were mad to sell at any price, but there were no buyers. In less time than it takes to write about it the price fell from 162 to 135. The great gigantic gold bubble had burst, and half Wall Street was involved in ruin."

Congress upon assembling in December promptly ordered an investigation as to the cause of the disaster. It could not well do otherwise, the Treasury having entered Wall Street to control the gold market in the interest of the bears. Nothing came from the investigation, however, except two reports from the committee appointed to do the work, the opinions of the members being divided on the subject according to their political predilections, and the Treasury resumed the ordinary sales of gold.

In February, 1873, another coinage act was passed, making the gold dollar the standard unit of account, but no change was made in the weight or fineness of the gold coins. It authorized, however, the coinage of the gold dollar and three dollar pieces, and made all gold coins of the United States a full legal tender in all payments when not below the standard weight and limit of tolerance, as therein provided for each piece, and when below such standard and tolerance to be a legal tender at valuation in proportion to their actual weight; "And any gold coin of the United States, if reduced in weight by natural abrasion, not more than one-half of one per centum below the standard weight prescribed by law, after a circulation of twenty years, as shown by its date of coinage, and at a ratable proportion for any period less than twenty years, shall be received at their nominal value by the United States Treasury," &c.

The standard weight of a gold dollar was fixed at 25.8 grains troy. The deviation allowed by law in adjusting the weight of gold coins was to be, in the double eagle and the eagle one-half of a grain, and in the other coins one-fourth of a grain for each piece. Precisely at what point one of these coins through abrasion ceases to be a legal tender, or not receivable at the Treasury, becomes under the law an interesting question in vulgar fractions, and, when ascertained, the possessor would require a nicely adjusted scale to make his information of any service.

Congress borrowed this provision of the coinage act from England, in which country it had for some time existed. When first put into operation in that country considerable attention was paid to its provisions, and society ladies took pride in being able to tell precisely how much any worn coin was worth. Miniature scales accurately adjusted and highly ornamented were manufactured for the purpose, and ladies wore them hung about their necks. These scales are now frequently met with in pawn-shops and second-hand jewelry establishments. No attention is now paid to the complicated requirements of the act, however, except by the Bank of England; and coins, however much worn, pass readily at their nominal value, only the ignorant and the unwary ever presenting a doubtful piece at the counters of that institution.

The coinage act of 1873 also directed that all coins in the Treasury below legal weight should be recoined, and in accordance therewith light coins, representing in nominal value upwards of $25,000,000, were recoined into full-weight pieces at an expense of about $100,000. As nearly all the coin in the country was at that time held by the Treasury, but few light-weight pieces in existence escaped the melting-pot, and consequently the gold coins now in circulation are but little worn or defaced.

Upon the resumption of specie payments in January, 1879, a vast amount of gold coin returned to this country from Europe, where it had been driven by the paper issues of the government. Since that time the gold dollar has been maintained as a standard of value and a unit of account. Owing to the prevalence of notes of small denomination, however, but little gold appears in circulation.

As a monetary standard gold is as good, if not better, than silver. For fifty years it has maintained an exchange power for other commodities of surprising uniformity, and during the same period the average wages in all occupations have more than doubled, while the price of silver has decreased 25 per cent. The report of the Senate Finance Committee on wholesale prices and wages, 1893, gives the price of eighty-five articles of ordinary consumption in gold for every year from 1840 to 1891, and the ratio of wages in gold of all occupations for the same period, those for 1860 in each case being reckoned as 100. Mr. Augustus Sauerbeck, an Englishman, has also published recently the results of his investigations as to the yearly London prices of forty-five commodities, and of silver, from 1850 to 1891. Omitting 1870 prices, as at that time they were affected by the circulation of depreciated paper, the information may be tabulated as follows, for the end of each decade:

	SENATE COMMITTEE.		SAUERBECK.	
YEAR.	Average relative price of 85 principal articles.	Average relative wages all occupations.	Average relative prices of 45 principal articles.	Average relative price of silver.
1840......	98.5	82.5		98.7
1850......	92.6	90.9	77.	102.0
1860......	100.0	100.0	99.	99.6
1880......	103 04	143.0	88.	85.0
1891......	96.2	168.6	72.	74.1

It will be seen that the value of gold in exchange for the average of eighty-five articles has varied for fifty-one years less than four per cent; that wages have more than doubled meanwhile. The wage-earners certainly have no cause for complaint. Silver since 1860 has shrunk 25 per cent in a like comparison, owing mainly to its largely increased production.

The relative value of gold, like that of any other commodity, will depend upon its demand and supply, and there is nothing in the annual yield of that metal to indicate any scarcity of it in the future.

The following carefully prepared table shows the value of the world's product of the two metals for the year 1800 and each succeeding tenth year to 1890, and for 1893, total and per 100, computed on the population of America and Europe. It will be seen that the world's production of gold alone in 1893 was but little less than that of both metals in 1870, and that its per capita production was greater in 1893 than for both metals at any period previous to 1860.

Years.	Population Europe and America.	Gold.	Silver (coining value).	Total.	Rate per 100 of Population.		
					Gold.	Silver.	Total.
1800	197,505,895	*$11,823,000	*$36,540,000	*$48,363,000	$5.99	$18.50	$24.49
1810	215,397,857	*11,815,200	*37,167,700	*48,982,900	5.49	17.26	22.74
1820	244,712,906	* 7,606,300	*22,478,600	*30,084,900	3.11	9.19	12.29
1830	269,183,091	* 9,447,900	*19,144,400	*28,592,300	3.51	7.11	10.62
1840	294,121,654	*13,484,100	*24,793,000	*38,277,100	4.58	8.43	13.01
1850	317,323,176	44,450,000	39,000,000	83,450,000	14.01	12.29	26.29
1860	346,325,438	119,250,000	40,800,000	160,050,000	34.43	11.78	46.21
1870	378,697,628	106,850,000	51,575,000	158,425,000	28.21	13.62	41.83
1880	424,900,038	106,500,000	96,700,000	203,200,000	25.06	22.76	47.81
1890	466,789,341	118,849,000	172,235,000	291,084,000	25.46	36.90	62.36
1893	†480,582,966	157,228,000	209,165,000	366,393,000	32.72	43.52	76.24

* One-tenth of production of decade. No report by years.
† Estimated.

If there is any advantage in a silver standard over that of gold, it should appear in the prices of labor and commodities in the countries thus employing silver. The republic of Mexico adjoins that of the United States. Both countries are producers of the two metals, yet in Mexico the ordinary farm laborer lives in an adobe house of one room, and receives for his services about twelve cents of our money per day, on which he must live. From official sources furnished by the

Bureau of American Republics, the following tables have been compiled, the first showing the rate of wages in the city of Mexico in 1890, compared with those of the United States at the same time, viz.:

OCCUPATIONS.	WAGES IN MEXICO PER DAY.		WAGES IN UNITED STATES PER DAY.	Difference in favor of the United States.
	Mexican silver dollar.	Equivalent in United States gold coin.	Gold coin or its equivalent.	
Blacksmiths	$2.50	$1.88	$2.50	$ .62
Carpenters	1.50	1.13	2.55	1.42
Quarrymen	.50	.38	1.50	1.12
Railroad contractors,	1.00	.75	3.84	3.09
Stone-cutters	1.25	.94	3.50	2.56
Tinners	.875	.66	2.45	1.99
House-painters	1.25	.98	2.28	1.30
Gas-fitters	1.00	.75	1.97	1.22
Printers	2.00	1.50	2.50	1.00
Coach-makers	2.00	1.50	2.50	1.00
Weavers	1.00	.75	1.30	.55
Pattern-makers	1.25	.94	3.24	2.30
Machinists	1.75	1.31	2.44	1.13
Engine-drivers	1.50	1.13	3.79	2.66
Firemen	1.50	1.13	2.00	.89

The second table shows that at the same time the prices of nearly all the commodities mentioned were higher in Mexico than in the United States, viz.:

COMMODITIES.	PRICES IN MEXICO.		PRICES IN THE UNITED STATES.	In favor of United States.
	Mexican dollar.	Equivalent in United States gold.	(Gold.)	
Flour, per bbl.	$10.780	$8.080	$5.100	$2.980
Sugar, per lb.	.190	.140	.050	.090
Coffee, per lb.	.740	.180	.200	*.020
Beans, per lb.	.500	.380	.500	*.120
Rice, per lb.	.085	.063	.055	.008
Lard, per lb.	.18	.135	.060	.075
Ham, per lb.	.30	.225	.114	.115
Cheese, per lb.	.25	.187	.100	.087

* In favor of Mexico.

There is nothing in these tables to indicate that the wage-earner is better off in Mexico with its free silver than in the United States on a gold basis; but there is everything to indicate that his condition is not nearly so good; which condition is generally admitted, whatever may be its cause.

CHAPTER XX.

THE SILVER DOLLAR.

The Spanish milled dollar, or, more strictly speaking, the Mexican pillar-piece, was a popular coin among the colonists. The British mint declared in 1707 that it contained $386\frac{5}{8}$ grains of pure silver. By the British standard at that time 444 grains of such silver was rated at 62 pence. Consequently the dollar contained 54 pence. A pound sterling contained 240 pence, and was therefore worth $4.44\frac{4}{9}$ of those dollars, and this valuation of the pound sterling continued as an assumed value until January 1, 1873, notwithstanding that meanwhile both the pound and the dollar had been subjected to many important changes.

In the year 1772 the amount of pure silver in the dollar was by law reduced to $377\frac{1}{4}$ grains. In 1785 the Congress of the Confederation adopted the dollar as a unit of account, declaring that it contained 375.64 grains of pure silver.

In 1792 Congress passed an act establishing for the country a uniform money of account, with this dollar for a unit, declaring that it should contain 371¼ grains of pure, or 416 grains of standard silver. The same act also provided that 24.73 grains of pure gold should be the legal equivalent of this dollar, and that, in all coined pieces, one pound of pure gold should be deemed equivalent to fifteen pounds of pure silver.

The legal relation between the two metals of 1 to 15 thus established proved to be a close approximation to the commercial one existing at that time. If anything, gold was for a short time a little undervalued, yet but little of it came to the mint for coinage. Foreign gold coins, to which the people were accustomed, furnished a satisfactory medium for making coin exchanges. Their values were reckoned in shillings and pence, and the new money of account, with its dollars, its decimal divisions and multiples, for a long time met with but little favor.

The gold and silver coins were full legal tender for their face value in the payment of all debts, but their paper representatives, though often much depreciated below their face value, constituted much of the circulating medium of the country, although not endowed with any legal tender power.

Soon after the passage of the Coinage Act, silver became comparatively cheaper than gold, and a considerable amount of it found its way to the mint for coinage. In 1809 one pound of gold was worth in the market 16½ pounds of silver.

The legal relation, however, remained unchanged between the two metals. Gold therefore became a commodity, and the small amount coined was shipped abroad to pay for imported goods. Silver had meanwhile superseded gold as a circulating medium, and its comparative cheapness stimulated its coinage.

The silver dollar was now the unquestioned unit of account, and in silver coins all contracts calling for dollars could be satisfied. Mr. Jefferson, who was then President, had favorably indorsed the ratio of 1 to 15 proposed by Mr. Hamilton, and adopted in the coinage act of 1792. He believed that both metals could and would circulate side by side under the relation fixed by that act.

But it was discovered that while the mint was coining silver as rapidly as its horse-power machinery would permit, none of the dollar pieces came into circulation, and that the bullion presented for silver coinage consisted mainly of Spanish silver dollars. This unexpected result arose from the exchange of our dollars in the West Indies and Mexico at par for the Spanish dollars. The natives of those countries, thinking that a dollar was a dollar if declared so by a government, let go their own piece for another three grains lighter. Thus did the wily Quaker banker of Philadelphia wheedle a good percentage out of his less favored brother. It was not the first time rapacious bankers had made money out of the ignorant through monetary legislation, and probably it will not be the last. We should not be, however, too ready to smile at the simplicity of the Spanish-American population. Even the justices of the Supreme Court of the United States as late as 1873 declared a doctrine in the legal tender case of wonderfully the same import.

The further exportation of silver dollars for the benefit of Quaker bankers, however, was soon brought to an end. In 1806 President Jefferson, who believed that both gold and silver would circulate upon equal terms if properly regulated, stopped the coinage of dollars by an order issued through the State Department, as follows:

DEPARTMENT OF STATE, May 1, 1806.

SIR: In consequence of a representation from the director of the Bank of the United States, that considerable purchases have been made of dollars coined at the mint for the purpose of exporting them, and as it is probable further purchases and exportations will be made, the President directs that all the silver to be coined at the mint shall be of small denominations, so that the value of the largest pieces shall not exceed half a dollar.

I am, etc.,

JAMES MADISON.

ROBERT PATTERSON, ESQ.,
Director of the Mint.

At that time there had been coined of silver dollars 1,439,457 pieces.

The coinage of the silver dollar was not resumed until 1836.

The operations under the ratio of 1 to 15 gradually expelled gold from circulation, and, the coinage of the silver dollar being prohibited, the worn fractional Spanish pieces made legal tender by the act of 1793 furnished to a great extent the circulation of the country, with bank notes for use in large transactions. The objections to these notes have already been stated.

The monetary condition grew worse with time, and in 1830 the House of Representatives referred to a special committee of that body petitions and memorials asking for relief therefrom. Mr. Campbell P. White, of New York, was made chairman of the committee, which for two sessions carefully considered all projects looking to a reform of the currency. Three reports were made. In one the committee, after submitting some coinage tables, says: " From these statements it appears that the mint has coined since its establishment in 1794 about $37,000,000, of which about four-fifths probably have been exported, leaving only seven to eight millions in the United States, after incurring the heavy expenditure of nearly one million dollars." This was the net result of the free coinage of both metals for fifty years.

That the condition of the currency was unsatisfactory was everywhere admitted, but as to the remedy therefor, there arose disagreements among the political doctors. This committee, after pondering profoundly through an entire session of Congress, concluded that the fault was in the ratio, and to the ratio the remedy must be applied. The Secretary of the Treasury had recommended 1 to 15.625, and this after much deliberation was accepted by the committee as the ratio desired — just why does not very clearly appear, but the committee had been considering the matter so long it evidently thought it better to suggest something, and if the ratio did not prove satisfactory the blame could be put upon the Secretary, who had recommended it. Nobody seemed to have had any opinion as to the probable result, but one thing was certain — if any change occurred it could hardly be for the worse. A bill fixing the ratio at 1 to 15.625 passed through the committee of the whole, and doubtless would have passed the House without much opposition, but at this juncture a political breeze struck it as before stated. The issues of the banks had become very obnoxious to a large class of persons, and a determined effort was on foot to rid the country of their circulation. There was also a decided opposition to the further continuance of the United States Bank, with its thirteen million dollars of notes. In the Senate

Thomas H. Benton led the opposition, and it was known that he was acting in full sympathy with the administration. It was alleged that by increasing the ratio, gold would circulate and eventually drive out the bank notes. Of course no such result would come, for notes will circulate on any metallic basis, or perhaps on none at all, with equal facility; but the extinction of the notes was the end in view, and gold was to be the means employed to accomplish it. For that purpose a ratio of 1 to 16 was accepted by the friends of the administration. The object of the change Mr. Benton distinctly said was:

> To enable the friends of gold to go to work at the right place to effect the recovery of that precious metal which their fathers once possessed, which the subjects of European kings now possess, which the citizens of the young republics now possess, but which the yeomanry of this America have been deprived of for more than twenty years, and will be deprived of forever unless they discover the cause of the evil and apply the remedy to its root.

One to 16 became a party cry. There was no resisting the popular demand. Mr. White faced about and moved an amendment to his own bill making the ratio 1 to 16, the gold to be reduced about 1½ grains to a dollar, the silver to remain unchanged in weight. He had admitted that the ratio before recommended was the utmost limit to which it could be extended with safety to silver, and must have known that the new ratio would in effect demonetize that metal. The bill as amended passed the House 145 to 36, even John Quincy Adams giving it his support. In the Senate it was discussed but little, passing by a vote of 35 to 7, Daniel Webster voting for it, Henry Clay against it. President Jackson gave it his approval June 28, 1834.

The Washington "Globe," in commenting upon the enactment of this measure, said:

> Contrary to their will the bank party even in the Senate have been obliged to vote for the measures of the administration deemed essential to carry out its policy. By public opinion they have been forced to vote for the *gold bill*, which is a measure of deadly hostility to the bank, will supersede its notes, and is the harbinger of a *real sound currency*. The people are now enabled to understand the policy of the administration, and to see that it would give them *gold* instead of *paper*.

If the policy of the administration was as asserted by the "Globe," to restore gold and drive out the notes, it was only partly successful. It brought gold into circulation, but not to the exclusion of notes. Silver, whatever may have been the purpose of the administration, was, however, shelved out of sight. In the final onslaught the white metal appears to have had no friend to wish it well as it departed. Its demonetization was practically as complete as though its coinage had been prohibited under penalty of death. Mr. White's committee did introduce a bill for the limited coinage of fractional silver pieces, purposely of light weight and of limited tender, to be used in making change and for small payments, but it never provoked a remark.

The bank did not obtain a new charter, and consequently its notes ceased to circulate, but not on account of the gold coinage. The State banks continued their issues which had various degrees of redeemability. To further aid the circulation of gold President Jackson, in 1836, issued an order under which public officers would receive only specie in payment of public dues.

The effect of the act of 1834, by which all silver was practically demonetized, soon began to be felt. Only Spanish silver pieces much worn could compete against the circulation of gold, reduced by the new ratio about seven per cent.

In 1846, by the passage of the Sub-Treasury Act, only specie could be received by the government on any account, and that received must be held until paid out by public officers, without depositing in a bank, thus increasing a demand for that kind of money, and in 1852 the Senate, upon the recommendation of R. M. T. Hunter, Chairman of the Finance Committee, passed a bill authorizing the Secretary of the Treasury to purchase silver bullion, and to coin it into fractional silver reduced about seven per cent in weight, the coins to be a legal tender for only five dollars, to be issued only at par in exchange for gold, and the profit on their coinage to accrue to the Treasury. Mr. Hunter claimed to be a bimetallist, to believe in the circulation of both gold and silver, but he could see no way to accomplish such a result except in the subordination of one metal to the other — in this case, of silver to gold. The financial condition of the country at that time under practical gold monometallism was little if any better than under that of silver monometallism in 1834, as will be seen by the following petition addressed to Congress by the Governor and members of the New Jersey Legislature:

To the Senate and House of Representatives of the United States in Congress assembled:

The memorial of the subscribers respectfully represents that the greatly increased value of silver compared with that of gold as regulated by law, at the Mint of the United States, *has almost wholly withdrawn all the silver coins of proper weight from circulation as a currency.* They are no longer a standard of value in payment, and are only used as an article of commerce.

Your honorable bodies are fully aware that the ordinary business of the community, comprising probably ninety-nine hundredths of all individual transactions, cannot be conducted without small coins, or paper tokens, to settle small balances; and however repugnant the use of such paper trash may be to the public opinion, or discreditable to the government and nation, the indispensable necessity for it will, as your memorialists seriously apprehend, soon force it upon the whole country, unless Congress shall, during the present session, provide an efficient remedy.

Your memorialists believe that such a remedy may be found in the passage of a bill that passed the Senate of the United States at their last session, which proposes a silver coinage about seven per cent lighter than the present coin, comprising all the existing denominations less than one dollar, and making these new coins a legal tender only for payments not exceeding five dollars.

In the House the measure was fully discussed. At most it only provided a limited amount of small silver for convenience in every-day transactions, but the discussion in the House shows that the practical demonetization of silver through the operations of the act of 1834 was known at that time, and that the gold standard was in general favor, and that nobody demanded the restoration of silver. Mr. Skelton, of New Jersey, remarked: "Gold is the only standard of value by which all property is now measured; it is virtually the only currency of the country." And again, in reference to another plan suggested: "We would thereby still continue the double standard of gold and silver, a thing the committee desires to obviate. They desire to have the standard currency to consist of *gold* only, and that these silver coins shall be entirely subservient to it, and that they shall be used rather as token than as standard currency."

Mr. Dunham, who had the measure in charge, said:

"Gentlemen talk about a double standard of gold and silver as a thing that exists, and that we propose to change. We have had but a single standard for the last three or four years. That has been, and now is, gold. We propose to let it remain so and to adapt silver to it, to regulate silver by it."

But little opposition was made to the measure, and it became a law February 21, 1853. Under its operations, halves, quarters, and dimes from our own mint began to appear in the circulation, much to the gratification of the country; and four years after, when the redemption of the worn foreign pieces had been accomplished, they met all the demands for a fractional coinage, to the great satisfaction of everybody. For the first time in the history of the country, we had a true bi-metallic currency, silver and gold circulating in harmony side by side. From no party or section came any cry that the silver dollar had been demonetized — nobody heard a whisper of the "stealthy crime" by which this coin had been prohibited.

The new scheme worked admirably. Everybody could get either silver or gold for labor or commodities, and the return to the free coinage of silver at a fixed ratio to gold was never once thought of until in 1876, when silver, mainly through the increased production, became the cheaper metal. But silver coins did not then put in an appearance, as was naturally expected. Congress in 1873 had passed an act revising the mint and coinage laws of the country, and had made no provisions for the further coinage of silver, except for the subsidiary pieces on government account. By the terms of that act, gold had become by law what it had been in fact since 1834, the legal standard of value, and this change was deliberately made with no prejudice to silver. Neither metal was then circulating save to a very limited extent; and there was nothing in the project except what had been advocated by the authors of the acts of 1834 and 1853 and generally accepted by the country. But the measure had been so roundly denounced as a crime, a *résumé* of the steps through which the bill passed before it became a law is presented.

On the 25th day of April, 1870, the Secretary of the Treasury sent to Congress a bill revising the laws relating to the mint, assay offices, and coinage of the United States, accompanied by a report giving a concise statement of the method adopted in preparing the bill, of the various amendments proposed to existing laws, and of the necessity for the changes recommended. In the letter of transmittal the Secretary stated that there had been no revision of the laws pertaining to the mint and coinage since 1837, and he expressed a belief that the passage of the bill enclosed would conduce greatly to the efficiency and economy of that important branch of the public service.

From the report it seems that in preparing the bill the existing laws pertaining to the matter were first arranged in a concise form, with such additional sections and suggestions as seemed valuable, and then submitted to the different mints and assay offices, to the officers of the Treasury Department familiar with coinage operations and the accounts arising therefrom, and to such other gentlemen as were known to be versed in metallurgical and numismatical subjects, with a request for such suggestions as experience and education should dictate; that in this way the views of more than thirty gentlemen, conversant with the manipulation of metals, the manufacture of coins, and the execution of laws pertaining thereto, were obtained; and that the bill was framed in accordance with these suggestions.

Among the amendments proposed to existing laws as set forth in the report, the important ones were the establishment of a Mint Bureau in the Treasury Department, to have charge of the operations of the mints and assay offices, and the discontinuance of the coinage of the silver dollar.

The reason given in the report for proposing the latter amendment was that, under the existing legal ratio between the two metals, the silver dollar was worth a premium in gold of about three and a half per centum, and that consequently the gold dollar was the unit of account, and no change therefrom was deemed advisable.

The appendix to the report also contained a marginal note, stating that the silver dollar was omitted from the bill. Subsequently, on June 25, 1870, the Secretary of the Treasury transmitted to the House of Representatives copies of the correspondence of the department, with the public officers and other gentlemen upon whose suggestions the bill had been framed, together with a letter from the Deputy Comptroller of the Currency, to whose supervision had been committed the preparation of the bill. Seven of these gentlemen discussed the proposition to discontinue the silver dollar, giving thereto their unqualified approval.

On December 9, 1870, the bill was reported from the Finance Committee of the Senate and printed with amendments.

On January 9, 1871, in accordance with previous notice, the bill came before the Senate, where it was discussed for two days and then passed.

On January 13, 1871, the House ordered the Senate bill to be printed. On February 25, 1871, the bill was reported from the Coinage Committee with an amendment, when it was again printed and recommitted. No further action on the bill was taken by Congress during that session.

On March 9, 1871, the bill was again introduced into the House and ordered to be printed. On January 9, 1872, Mr. Kelly, of Pennsylvania, Chairman of the Coinage Committee, reported the bill to the House with a recommendation that it pass. In his opening speech he said the bill had received as careful attention as he had ever known a committee to bestow on any measure. "We proceeded," he said, "with great deliberation to go over the bill, not only section by section, but line by line and word by word."

The bill, after considerable discussion, was again recommitted, again reported, again printed and recommitted, to be again reported and printed, and to be made the special order for March 12, 1872, until disposed of. An exhaustive discussion followed. Mr. Hooper, of Boston, in a carefully prepared speech of ten columns of the "Globe," explained the provisions of each section of the bill, and dwelt at length upon the proposition to discontinue the silver dollar. "This dollar," he said, "by reason of its intrinsic value being greater than its nominal value, long since ceased to be a coin of circulation, and is melted by manufacturers of silverware. It does not circulate in commercial transactions with any country, and the convenience of these manufacturers, in this respect, can better be met by supplying small stamped bars of the same standard, avoiding the useless expense of coining the dollar for that purpose."

Mr. Stoughton, of the Coinage Committee, expressed like views.

Mr. Potter, of New York, spoke of the change proposed, whereby the legal tender coin of the country would consist of one metal instead of two, and said: "I think this would be a wise provision, and that the full legal tender coins should be of gold alone."

Mr. Kelly also said: "It is impossible to retain the double standard. The values of gold and silver continually fluctuate. . . . Hence all experience has shown that you must have one standard coin which shall be a full legal tender, and then you may promote your domestic convenience by having a subsidiary coinage of silver which shall circulate in all parts of your country as legal tender for a limited amount."

On May 27, 1872, the bill passed the House, — yeas, 110; nays, 13.

So far as it related to the silver coinage, it was identical with the bill prepared at the Treasury, with the exceptions that it provided for the coinage of a silver dollar weighing 384 grains, and made all the silver coins a legal tender for $5 in any one payment, instead of for all sums less than $1. This dollar would be but the weight of two half dollars, and was designed to be coined only on government account, as were the fractional pieces.

Just before the passage of the bill, Mr. McNeeley, of the Coinage Committee, said he had carefully examined every line of the bill, and, understanding the subject, he was satisfied that the bill ought to pass.

The bill was again printed in the Senate, and referred to the Committee on Coinage. Subsequently, upon being again reported from that committee, it was again printed. Further amendments were proposed, and it was again printed with the amendments, and, after a discussion occupying nineteen columns of the "Congressional Globe," it passed the Senate.

The bill was sent to the House, where it was again printed and referred to a Committee of Conference, which finally agreed as to its form, and the bill as reported from the conference became a law February 12, 1873.

In place of the subsidiary dollar of 384 grains, with a limited legal tender quality, the Senate substituted a trade dollar weighing 420 grains, in accordance with the wishes of the dealers in bullion upon the Pacific Coast, that being considered as the most advantageous weight for a coin to be used for shipment to China and Japan.

The steps taken in framing and passing the act by which the coinage of the silver dollar was discontinued are herein so fully detailed because charges have frequently been made that the act was passed inadvertently or surreptitiously. As a final answer to such charges, it may be summed up that the bill was read in full in the Senate several times, and once, if not more, in the House; that it was printed by order of Congress thirteen times; that it was considered at length by the proper committees of both Houses during five different sessions, and that the debates on the bill in both Houses occupy 144 columns of the "Globe."

The passage of the act caused no material change in the coin circulation of the country. Since 1806 no silver dollars had been coined for circulation, and the small amount, if any, which had ever entered into circulation had long before disappeared. Yet the act took from these dollars, if any there were, none of the properties they ever possessed. They were still a full legal tender in the payment of debts.

Hardly had the coinage act of 1873 gone into effect, discontinuing the free coinage of silver, when the metal, as compared with gold, fell rapidly in price. In less than twelve months thereafter, the amount of silver required for the coinage of a full weight dollar could be purchased in the market for 98 cents in gold. In 1875 it could be purchased for 94 cents; in 1876 for ,79.2 cents; in 1877 for 90 cents; in 1880 for 87½ cents; in 1885 for 80 cents; in 1890 for 74 cents, and in 1893 for 51 cents — the most violent fluctuation in the relative values of the two metals of which history gives any record.

Many causes combined to produce this fluctuation, some of which are well known. The extraordinary yield of silver in Nevada had increased the stock on hand. The German government had, in 1871, undertaken to redeem the enormous amount of silver coin circulating in that empire, and to replace it with gold coin, the silver redeemed to be melted down and sold at the best rates obtainable. Through this operation over seven million pounds of pure silver had been thrown into the market. Alarmed at the abundance of this metal, the Netherlands changed their coins from silver to gold, and the Latin Union — composed of France, Italy, Belgium, Switzerland, and Greece — in 1874 suspended the coinage of silver throughout the Union, and steps to that end were taken by other countries.

Had the coming disparity in the relation between the two metals been foreseen, the action of Congress in 1873, establishing a single gold standard, would, in view of the action of European governments, have been considered as conservative and judicious legislation by many well versed in monetary affairs.

By maintaining the gold dollar as a unit of account, Congress kept the circulating medium of this country in harmony with that of Europe, thus saving to the producers in this country heavy premium charges in effecting exchanges, which bankers would have been compelled to impose to protect themselves against loss from the constantly changing relation of the two metals.

Had silver not been discontinued, its coinage at the mint for purposes of circulation would have been resumed upon the fall in price of silver bullion, and resumption of specie payments would have occurred probably in 1876 upon a silver basis twenty per cent below that of gold, with only silver coins — the dollar issued for depositors under the original coinage act, and fractional pieces issued under the act of 1853 on government account — of different denomination and of different weight and debt-paying power. Public, state, municipal, corporate, and private indebtedness, contracted prior to the change of standard and payable in coin, would then have been satisfied by the payment of these silver coins, as they had a legal if not an actual existence at the time the obligations were contracted. Nor would the debtor have had, in such an event, any just ground of complaint. No one had ever alleged of either metal an immutability of value, and the obligee to a contract calling for "coin" took a risk, which he was presumed to know, of being paid in the cheaper metal.

The discontinuance of free silver, however, took from the obligor the power, if not the right, to satisfy his coin obligations by payment in silver dollars. The number of private contracts in the country affected by such discontinuance was probably not great, or their amount excessive; but a large amount of corporate, municipal, state, and national indebtedness existed, payable in coin, and contracted previously to 1873, and this could now be paid only in gold.

A large portion of the national debt contracted during the rebellion called only for "dollars," and not without reason there had arisen in the country a considerable demand that these obligations should be satisfied with United States notes, those being the kind of dollars the government received for the obligations. To explain the meaning of previous legislation, Congress in 1869 had pledged the faith of the United States to the payment in coin or its equivalent of all the obligations of the government, except in cases where the authorizing act expressly provided that payment therefor might be made in other money than gold and silver. Subsequently the issue of bonds for refunding purposes was authorized, but in this case the act of authorization specifically provided that the bonds should be redeemable in coin of the then existing standard value. The act was approved July 14, 1870, at which time the silver dollar had an existence in the public statutes, and of course neither its discontinuance, nor the great fall in the price of silver bullion, was contemplated or foreseen.

While these changes in the coinage laws were being made, and the relative values of silver and gold were so rapidly fluctuating, the country was employing for a circulating medium only United States notes and the issues of the national banks, and current exchanges were consequently not affected to any appreciable extent by the fluctuating ratio between the two metals. Gold continued to be employed in payment of customs dues and interest on the public debt as before, and nobody felt wronged.

But the same class of men that had sought to pay the public debt in depreciated paper, and had been defeated by the act of 1869, now saw another opportunity to lessen the obligations of the government. The restoration of silver to the place it occupied previously to its discontinuance in 1873 would at once make the silver dollar the unit of account, and as soon as a supply of silver coins could be issued from the mint, payments on account of interest or principal of the public debt would be made in silver instead of gold, a saving from twenty to forty-five per cent in all payments thus made. They asserted that no repudiation was involved in the transaction, silver as well as gold being the coin "nominated in the bond." Legally the position was well taken, and the government had only to consider what in equity was due to the holders of public notes and bonds, and whether it could afford to take advantage of its technical right to pay its debt with the depreciated metal. The larger portion of the debt had been contracted when gold was the only coin in circulation, and holders of the public securities naturally supposed that the securities would eventually be paid in gold. To pay them in a cheaper metal would subject the government to the charge of a partial repudiation of its indebtedness. This charge would be unjust, but no explanation would ever fully satisfy the world that the government had acted wholly in good faith in thus returning to a silver basis to take advantage of its creditors.

As for the silver dollar piece it had never formed any essential part of the metallic circulation of the country, and its discontinuance attracted no attention for some time. Occasional mention of its absence was made in the public press, in connection with the rapid decline of the price of silver bullion in 1875 and 1876. No demand for its restoration was urged, and the question of its further coinage formed no part of the issues on which were conducted the local and national campaigns in the autumn of the last-named year.

In the House of Representatives on March 25, 1875, Mr. Reagan had offered an amendment to a bill to provide for the issue of small silver coins, declaring that the silver coins of the United States of the denomination of one dollar should be a legal tender in any one payment at their nominal value, for any amount not exceeding $50. This amendment was agreed to. The only effect of the proposed change was to increase the legal tender power of the trade dollar, that being the only dollar coin either authorized or fabricated. But in the Senate, a month later, the amendment was changed so as to provide for the coinage of a silver dollar nine-tenths fine, to weigh $412\frac{8}{10}$ grains troy, and to be a legal tender for any amount not exceeding $20 in any one payment, except for customs dues and interest on the public debt. This dollar was not to be coined for depositors of bullion, but only upon government account, the profit in its issue to accrue to the public Treasury. Nothing came, however, of either proposition.

The session of Congress following the presidential campaign of 1876 was occupied principally in determining the succession to the presidency, and pending that controversy little attention was paid to the monetary affairs of the country, in Congress or elsewhere. That matter settled, the proposed remonetization of silver at once became a disturbing element in local and national politics. The newly-made friends of that metal became very numerous and unnecessarily noisy. They alleged that designing men had surreptitiously secured the passage of the act prohibiting free silver, although one of their number had in the House advocated the passage of the act, and especially commended the provision for such prohibition.

They attributed to the absence of a silver coinage the disasters following the panic of 1873, although up to the time of that panic, even had there been no adverse legislation, silver coins would not have appeared in circulation, owing to the high price of silver bullion. They euphoniously spoke of the "dollar of our daddies," and alleged that, in discontinuing it, an indignity had been heaped upon the worthy founders of the republic, although an equal distribution of all silver dollars coined would not have given one piece to every ten voters when Jefferson stopped its coinage.

In the press, on the platform, and in Congress, they pictured the distress the poor man had suffered through the alleged mischievous legislation, and stoutly demanded the restoration of the coin as a panacea for all the evils, real or imaginary, with which the country was afflicted. With unsparing epithets they denounced those who had invested their earnings in public securities as "leeches," "bloated bondholders," "vampires, flapping their dragon wings over a ruined country," and hinted that, unless the coin was restored to circulation, communism and anarchy would follow. One over-zealous Congressman openly asserted that, unless the public debt was paid in silver, he and his friends would rise in their might and wipe out the entire debt as with a sponge.

In May, 1877, the legislature of Illinois determined that the evils resulting from the discontinuance of the silver coinage should be remedied, as far as within its power, and as there were no full weight silver coins in the country, and the State had no power to coin any, it resorted to the unhappy device of declaring the halves, quarters, and dimes a full legal tender for the payment of debts within that State. The measure was promptly vetoed by the governor, and the State was thus spared any further humiliation from the action of its too zealous legislators.

The restoration of silver to its former place as an alternative with gold was generally demanded throughout the country, without distinction of party. The Republicans of Ohio, in convention,

August, 1877, demanded the remonetization of silver, but with coinage and valuation so regulated that our people should not be placed at a disadvantage in their trade with foreign nations, and that both metals should be kept in circulation, as contemplated by the Constitution. About the same time the Democrats of that State in convention denounced the demonetization of silver as an outrage upon the rights of the people, although no member of the convention had probably ever seen a silver dollar at that time, except in a museum of curiosities, and for more than four years the "outrage" mentioned had been endured without being known.

The Republicans of Pennsylvania, a month later, thought that the long and successful existence of the double coin standard warranted them in demanding a repeal of the legislation which had demonetized silver and established "an almost exclusive gold standard," and a return to the free use and unrestricted coinage of the silver dollar, thus preserving the equality of the commercial value of the silver dollar with the gold dollar, and keeping both in circulation. With sop of this diluted character both parties fed their adherents through the campaigns of that year.

The Forty-fourth Congress having adjourned without making the annual appropriation for the support of the army, President Hayes called an extra session of that body to convene October 16, 1877; and on November 5, Representative Bland, of Missouri, moved to suspend the rules and pass a bill directing the coinage of silver dollars of the weight of 412½ grains standard silver, as provided in the act of January 18, 1837, the coins to be a legal tender at their nominal value for all debts and dues, public and private, except where otherwise provided by contract, and providing that any owner of silver bullion might deposit the same at the mints to be coined into such dollars for his benefit, upon the same terms and conditions as gold bullion. This was agreed to, — yeas, 164; nays, 34; not voting, 92.

This bill, if it had become a law, would have restored the double standard; and as the silver bullion necessary for a dollar could have been purchased in the market for eighty-five cents in gold, every person, corporation, or State, owing debts payable in coin, would have been enabled to satisfy such obligations at a discount of fifteen per cent. from their face value, as soon as a sufficient amount of the coins for the purpose could have been put into circulation.

The passage of the bill in the House was received with general satisfaction throughout the country, the masses of the people believing that with cheaper money good times would come. Any question of political or personal integrity involved in the scheme was little considered.

On November 21, in the Senate, Mr. Allison, from the Committee on Finance, reported the bill with several important amendments. The authority for owners of silver bullion to have dollars coined therefrom for their benefit was stricken out, and, instead, the Secretary of the Treasury was authorized, and directed, out of any money in the Treasury not otherwise appropriated, to purchase, from time to time, silver bullion at the market price, not less than two million dollars nor more than four million dollars per month, and to have it coined into such dollars as fast as purchased, the gain arising from the transaction to be paid into the Treasury.

The bill thus amended gave to the government alone the right to pay coin obligations at the rate of eighty-five cents on a dollar, because the coins manufactured would be sold by the mints to other parties only at their face valuation in gold.

No action upon the proposition was taken during the extra session. Upon the assembling of Congress in December, President Hayes, in his annual message, recommended the limited coinage of silver dollars of increased weight, with a proviso that in no case should the then outstanding public debt ever be paid in any coinage of less commercial value than the gold coin as it then existed. No heed was paid to his recommendations; the Allison amendment was adopted by the Senate and concurred in by the House, by large majorities. The bill was however vetoed by the President, but upon its return to Congress became a law February 28, 1878, notwithstanding the veto, more than two-thirds of each House voting in its favor.

Before the passage of the bill two sections had been added; one directing the President, immediately upon the passage of the act, to invite the governments of the countries comprising the "Latin Union," and of such other European nations as he might deem advisable, to join the United States in a conference to adopt a common ratio between gold and silver for the purpose of establishing, internationally, the use of bimetallic money, and securing fixity of relative values between the two metals, and to appoint commissioners for that purpose; the other authorized the holders of the silver dollars to deposit them in the Treasury in sums not less than ten dollars, and to receive therefor certificates, the coin to be held for the redemption of the certificates, and the certificates to be receivable for customs, taxes, and all public dues, and when so received to be reissuable.

The coinage of the silver dollar under this act was at once resumed, a comparatively small number of the pieces were put into circulation and that at great expense. Certificates for their deposit were issued, however, each bearing on its face this legend: "This certifies that there has been deposited in the Treasury of the United States —— silver dollars, payable to the bearer on demand;" on its back the following: "This certificate is receivable for customs taxes and all public dues, and when received may be reissued." The certificates readily passed as money.

The demand for a restoration of silver as a standard of value, however, was what the sudden demand for silver meant. To partly appease this demand, Mr. Conger, in the House of Representatives, January 20, 1890, introduced a bill authorizing the issue of notes upon deposits of silver bullion. On June 7 a substitute to same end, which had been agreed upon in a Republican caucus, was presented and adopted. On June 18 the Senate passed a substitute for the substitute, providing, among other things, for the free coinage of silver at the former ratio of 1 to 16. A conference committee on the disagreements of the two Houses was appointed, and it agreed upon a measure understood to have been drawn by Senator Sherman, which provided for the purchase of 4,500,000 ounces of silver bullion each month, at the market price, for which should be issued Treasury notes, legal tender in payment of all debts, public and private, except where otherwise expressly stipulated in the contract; to be redeemable at the discretion of the Secretary of the Treasury in gold or silver coin, " it being the established policy of the United States to maintain the two metals at a parity with each other upon the present legal ratio, or such ratio as may be provided by law."

This bill was approved July 14, 1890, and became known as the Sherman act. Operations thereunder were promptly carried into effect, the act superseding that of 1878.

In the summer of 1893, the country was again in the throes of a monetary panic, and the President summoned Congress to a special session. He urgently recommended the repeal of the Sherman act, as under its provisions all the silver certificates of 1878, treasury notes of 1890, as well as the United States notes, were by implication redeemable in gold, if the parity of the two metals were to be maintained; and the reserve of $100,000,000 accumulated for the redemption of United States notes, but now used against a circulation of $900,000,000, and also believed to be liable for current demands, constituted such an element of weakness that apprehensions were felt as to the ability of the government to maintain the parity called for, at least without either an increase of the reserve or a reduction in the obligations against it. After a long discussion the repeal was effected, November 1, 1893, and no further purchases of silver have since been made. Under the operations of the two acts, silver has been purchased as follows: Under the act of 1878, 291,272,019 fine ounces at a cost of $308,279,261; under that of 1890, 168,674,682 ounces at a cost of $155,931,002. The silver bullion purchased would have a coinage value of about $590,000,000. It would sell to-day with silver at 67 cents an ounce for only about $328,000,000, or $136,000,000 less than paid for it by the government, and this latter amount is the cost to government from yielding even partly to the demands for free silver, and going into banking operations as a compromise.

CHAPTER XXI.

MONETARY CONFERENCES.

FORESEEING the difficulties which would follow the attempted introduction of the silver dollar into the currency at the proposed fictitious valuation, Congress, in the act of 1878, which again authorized the manufacture of this coin, directed the President to invite the governments of the so-called Latin Union,* and such other European nations as he might deem advisable, to join the United States in a conference, with a view to the adoption of a common ratio between gold and silver, "for the purpose of establishing internationally the use of bi-metallic money and securing fixity of relative value between these metals."

---

* France, Italy, Belgium, and Switzerland had, in 1865, formed what was known as the Latin Union, entering into an agreement by which the amount of silver to be coined each year was fixed for each member of the Union. The coins were to be of like character, and to be received without discrimination throughout the Union, both on public and private account. Greece joined the Union in 1868. In 1874, by mutual agreement, the coinage of silver was suspended throughout the Union.

In pursuance of these directions, the President invited European nations to send delegates to meet the delegates of the United States in Paris in conference for the purpose mentioned. The delegates selected, and who went to that city from the United States, were Hon. R. E. Fenton, Hon. W. S. Groesbeck, Prof. Francis A. Walker, and Prof. S. Dana Horton, gentlemen well known in political and scientific circles.

The European nations invited who sent delegates to the convention, were Austria-Hungary, Belgium, France, Great Britain, Greece, Italy, the Netherlands, Russia, Sweden, Norway, and Switzerland. Germany, although invited, declined to send.

The delegates assembled in Paris August 10, 1878, in accordance with the invitations, and Mr. Leon Say, the French Minister of Finance, was elected president of the convention.

From the report of the proceedings it seems that the several nations represented in the convention were not favorably disposed to the reestablishment of the bi-metallic system.

The delegation from Austria-Hungary, in which country depreciated paper furnished almost exclusively the circulation, defended the bi-metallic system, but thought its adoption by that country at that time could not possibly have much effect.

The delegation from Belgium, a member of the

Latin Union, was very unfavorable to the proposed bi-metallic system.

France, a leading state of the Union, declared through her Finance Minister, the president of the conference, that in suspending the coinage of silver in 1874 she did not incline to the single gold standard, but, on the contrary, she occupied a position in which she might await a favorable moment to re-enter the system of the double standard, but offered little encouragement for any renewal of the double system at that time.

The delegates from Great Britain, which country had, since 1816, maintained an exclusively gold standard, expressed a willingness, and even a desire, that other nations should maintain a bi-metallic system, and give to silver the greatest possible circulation; but in their own country they said there was no disposition to use silver, except as a subordinate coin of a limited legal tender capacity.

The delegates from Greece appeared to be in sympathy with the views of France, and were willing to remain in a state of expectancy, hoping that other and greater nations might bring about the re-introduction of silver.

The delegates from Italy, another member of the Union, took advanced ground in defence of the bi-metallic system, but the circulation of that country being depreciated paper, the re-establishment of silver would, they thought, be of but little importance, there being no demand for silver for circulation.

The delegates from Holland declared that while England and Germany adhered to the gold monometallism, that country, standing between them both geographically and financially, must conform to their action.

The delegates from Russia announced the intention of that country to reserve its decision upon the question before the conference until such time as it should be prepared to resume specie payment.

The delegates from the government of Sweden and Norway announced that they had been appointed with instructions to refrain from participating in any measures which might compromise in any way the mono-metallic position of those States.

The delegates from Switzerland appeared as the uncompromising advocates of gold mono-metallism for Europe.

The Empire of Germany was not represented. At the second session the conference also invited that government to participate in its deliberations. This invitation, having been communicated to the ambassador of Germany, was declined, that nation having, after mature deliberation, but recently established the single gold standard.

Upon the assembling of the convention Mr.

Groesbeck, in behalf of the United States, stated the position of our government, making the following humiliating confession: —

"In 1873, in a law which did not very accurately carry out its purpose, silver was made to disappear through inadvertence rather than intentionally, by an omission to say anything about it. As a matter of fact, the silver standard was found to have been suppressed. The example of Germany had proved contagious; no newspaper had discussed the question; public opinion, by no means enlightened, was, so to speak, taken unawares, and great surprise was felt when, a short time after the law was passed, the change was fully perceived."

He closed by proposing that the conference should pronounce itself on the two following propositions: —

"1. It is the opinion of this assembly that it is not to be desired that silver should be excluded from free coinage in Europe and the United States of America. On the contrary, the assembly believe that it is desirable that the unrestricted coinage of silver, and its use as money of unlimited legal tender, should be retained where they exist, and, as far as practicable, restored where they have ceased to exist.

"2. The use of both gold and silver as unlimited legal tender money may be safely adopted; first, by equalizing them at a relation to be fixed by international agreement; and, secondly, by granting to each metal, at the relation fixed, equal terms of coinage, making no discrimination between them."

These propositions were discussed, but did not become the subject of a general vote. France, instead of supporting the delegates from the United States, as would naturally be expected of a country having so large an interest in the reinstatement of silver, joined with England in preparing an answer to be made by the European to the American delegates, which answer was adopted, as follows: —

"The delegates of the European states represented in the conference desire to express their sincere thanks to the government of the United States for having procured an international interchange of opinion upon a subject of so much importance as the monetary question.

"Having maturely considered the proposals of the representatives of the United States, they recognize, —

"1. That it is necessary to maintain in the world the monetary functions of silver, as well as those of gold, but that the selection for use of one or the other of the two metals, or of both simultaneously, should be governed by the special position of each state or group of states.

"2. That the question of the restriction of the coinage of silver should equally be left to the discretion of each state or group of states, according to the particular circumstances in which they may find themselves placed, and the more so in that the disturbance produced during the recent years in the silver market has variously affected the monetary situation of the several countries.

"3. That the differences of opinion which have appeared, and the fact that even some of the states which have the double standard find it impossible to enter into a mutual engagement with regard to the free coinage of silver, exclude the discussion of the adoption of a common ratio between the two metals."

In adopting these propositions, the delegates from America were treated more as messengers who had come across the water to submit a proposition to the conference, than as members of the conference and the representatives of the nation which had invited it. The European members withdrawing by themselves to vote upon the proposition, left the delegates from the United States to wait for an answer like criminals waiting for the verdict.

This action closed the conference, no result of any value having been obtained, and the delegates from the United States returned home to thus report.

For some time the matter rested, but the continued depression of the price of silver kept the subject under discussion, and in February, 1881, the governments of France and the United States extended joint invitations to the European nations to again take part in a conference with a view to establishing the use of gold and silver as international money.

The conference was to examine and "adopt, for the purpose of submitting the same to the governments represented, a plan and a system for the establishment, by means of an international agreement, of the use of gold and silver as bi-metallic money, according to a settled relative value between these two metals."

The conference assembled in Paris April 19, 1881. Delegates from the nations represented in the previous conference were present, and in addition thereto were delegates from Germany, British India, Denmark, and Portugal. The delegates representing the United States of America were Hon. William M. Evarts, Hon. Allen G. Thurman, Hon. Timothy O. Howe, and Prof. S. Dana Horton.

Mr. Magin, the French Minister of Finance, was elected president of the conference.

The sentiment in favor of a re-establishment of the bi-metallic system did not appear to have gained since the previous conference. Many of the delegates announced at once important reservations on their part. The delegates from Germany stated that between 1865 and 1870 a considerable quantity of gold had found its way into the treasury of the German Empire, and that that government had taken advantage of the occasion to firmly establish its monetary system upon the basis of a gold standard, and that this reform was now in a very advanced state. They also stated that there still remained in Germany at most only 500,000,000 marks in silver thalers, and declared that this reform had sensibly bettered the condition of the monetary circulation in Germany. Still, they had not failed to recognize the import of the fall of silver which had since occurred, and to relieve the Latin Union from the apprehension that this amount of marks, in old silver thalers, would be thrown upon the market as silver bullion, Germany had, in May, 1879, resolved to suspend its sales of silver, and they had not since been resumed. The delegates, however, recognized without reserve that a rehabilitation of silver was to be desired, and hoped that its free coinage might obtain in a certain number of the most populous states represented by the conference, but declared that Germany did not call for a change of system, and did not find herself in a position to concede the free coinage of silver. Still, having a disposition to assist the other powers which might unite for the purpose of a free coinage of silver at a fixed ratio with gold, Germany would agree for a period of some years to abstain from all sales of silver, and during another period of a certain duration would pledge itself to sell annually only a limited quantity, so small in amount that the general market would not be glutted thereby, and it would, perhaps, melt down and recoin 172,000,000 of old five-mark and two-mark silver pieces at a ratio between the two metals of about 1 to 15½, whereas the ratio then was 1 to 14. Stripped of all technical verbiage, the proposition was as if Germany should say, "Gentlemen of the other powers, believing you to be in earnest in your proposition to establish a fixed relative value between gold and silver, and that value to be as 1 to 15½, Germany offers her prayers for your success. She will not herself return to the free coinage of silver, but she will kindly hold 2,500 tons of old silver thalers, worth now about 77 per cent of their face value in gold, until, in accordance with your own theories, by your free coinage of silver you will force so much of that metal into new channels of circulation, that its price will be enhanced, and a fixed relation of equal value between gold and silver will be secured. When that time comes, we will unload our silver on you in exchange for gold at a profit of 30 per cent; and we are now prepared to discuss the details of the execution."

The delegate of Great Britain then followed, stating that for more than sixty years the monetary system of the United Kingdom had been with gold as a single standard, that this system had satisfied all the needs of the country, without giving rise to those disadvantages which had shown themselves elsewhere, and under other monetary regulations. That the government of Her Majesty could not, therefore, take part in a conference as supporting the principle of the double standard, but the representatives of the United States at London having declared that the powers represented at the conference reserved to themselves entire liberty of action after the discussion, the government of Her Majesty considered that it would be lacking in consideration towards friendly powers to persist in its refusal to send a delegate from the United Kingdom. That thus he had come, and that he stood ready to furnish any information desired concerning the monetary system of England, but he was not at liberty to vote upon any proposition which might be submitted to the conference. Subsequently he presented to the conference a communication from the Bank of England to the British government, setting forth to what extent the bank could aid the proposed league of countries for the rehabilitation of silver, which was in these words: —

"The Bank Charter Act permits the issue of

notes upon silver, but limits that issue to one-fourth of the gold held by the bank in the issue department.

"The purchase of gold bullion is obligatory and unlimited; the purchase of silver bullion is discretional and limited, the distinction being enforced by the necessity of paying notes in gold on demand.

"The re-appearance of silver bullion as an asset in the issue department of the Bank of England would, as is understood by the Foreign Office letter, depend entirely on the return of the mints of other countries to such rules as would insure the certainty of conversion of gold into silver, and silver into gold. The rules need not be identical with those formerly in force; the ratio between silver and gold, and the charge for mintage, may both or either of them be varied, and yet leave unimpaired the facility of exchange, which would be indispensable to the resumption of silver purchases by a bank of issue whose responsibilities are contracted in gold.

"Subject to these considerations, the Bank Court are satisfied that the issue of their notes against silver, within the letter of the act, would not involve the risk of infringing that principle of it which imposes a positive obligation on the bank to receive gold in exchange for notes, and to pay notes in gold on demand.

"The Bank Court see no reason why an assurance should not be conveyed to the monetary conference at Paris, if their lordships think it desirable, that the Bank of England, agreeably with the act of 1844, would be always open to the purchase of silver under the conditions above described."

The proposition of the Bank was a worthy rival of that of the delegates of Germany. In substance, the Bank proposed to accumulate silver in its vaults, worth in gold considerably less than its face value, so long as other countries than Great Britain would leave unimpaired the facilities of exchange, by which it could at any time obtain gold therefor, par for par, at a handsome profit.

The delegate from Denmark stated that the Danish government had no intention of abandoning the single gold standard introduced into the country a few years before, and that he had received instruction on the part of his government to abstain from all discussion of the manner in which the bi-metallic system could be regulated.

The delegate from Portugal frankly stated that the Portuguese monetary system then in force would not allow of its entry into the bi-metallic union then contemplated, and that he had no duty except to report to his government any action taken by the conference.

The delegate from Russia declared that the

Russian government reserved to itself entirely its right of opinion upon the whole matter, and in nothing renounced its liberty of action by reason of any resolution of the conference.

The delegate from Greece stated that his country had adopted mono-metallism, and he would not be able to join in any measure which might lead to a change in that system.

The delegate from Austria-Hungary stated his attitude to be one of friendly reserve, and that, if he thought proper to take part in the discussion, it would only be to express his personal opinions.

The delegates from Sweden and Norway announced that their countries had adopted a monetary union based upon a single standard of gold, but that they had been given permission to take part in the discussions, and to report to their respective governments.

The delegates of the Swiss Confederation announced that they should confine themselves to hearing the reasons which had moved the governments of the United States and France in calling the conference, but that they should not take part in any decision, of whatever nature it might be, without having first made a report to the Federal Council, and having received subsequent instructions from that body.

Notwithstanding these dispiriting responses, and especially those of the great powers of Germany and Great Britain, without whose aid there was no hope of securing bi-metallism, the conference proceeded to the discussion of the following propositions, which had been prepared for it by a committee of its own body: —

"1. Have the diminution and the great oscillations which have taken place in the value of silver, chiefly within the last few years, been hurtful or not to commerce, and consequently to general prosperity?

"Is it desirable that the relation of value between the two metals should possess a high degree of stability?

"2. Should the phenomena referred to in the first part of the preceding question be attributed to increase in the production of silver or to acts of legislation?

"3. Is it or is it not probable that, if a large group of states should agree to the free and unlimited mintage of lawful coins of the two metals, with full legal tender faculty at a uniform ratio between the gold and silver contained in the monetary unit of each metal, a stability in the relative value of these metals would be obtained, which, if not absolute, would at least be very substantial?

"4. If so, what measures should be taken to reduce to a minimum the oscillations in the relative value of the two metals?

"For instance: —

"1. Would it be desirable to impose upon privileged banks of issue the obligation to receive, at a fixed price, any gold and silver bullion which the public might offer?

"2. How could the same advantage be secured to the public in countries where privileged banks of issue do not exist?

"3. Should coinage be gratuitous, or at least uniform, for the two metals in all countries?

"4. Should there be an understanding that international trade in the precious metals should be left free of all restraint?

"5. In adopting bi-metallism, what should be the ratio between the weight of pure gold and of pure silver contained in the monetary units?"

On these propositions a long discussion ensued, eliciting much valuable information, but it seemed to be generally conceded that without the co-operation of Germany and Great Britain, which nations had been conspicuous in declining all propositions with a view of countenancing any hopes on their part of returning to the double standard, the convention must ultimately fail of its purpose.

As indicating more definitely the purpose of France and the United States, Mr. Evarts, in behalf of the delegates of those two countries, submitted, on the last day of the session, the following declaration: —

"The delegates of France and of the United States, in the name of their respective governments, make the following declarations: —

"1. The depreciation and great fluctuations in the value of silver, relatively to gold, which of late years have shown themselves, and which continue to exist, have been, and are, injurious to commerce and to the general prosperity, and the establishment and maintenance of a fixed relation of value between silver and gold would produce most important benefits to the commerce of the world.

"2. A convention, entered into by an important group of states, by which they should agree to open their mints to free and unlimited coinage of both silver and gold, at a fixed proportion of weight between the gold and silver contained in the monetary unit of each metal, and with full legal tender faculty to the money thus issued, would cause and maintain a stability in the relative value of the two metals suitable to the interests and requirements of the commerce of the world.

"3. Any ratio, now or of late in use by any commercial nation, if adopted by such important group of states, could be maintained; but the adoption of the ratio of 15½ to 1 would accomplish the principal object with less disturbance in the monetary systems to be affected by it than any other ratio.

"4. Without considering the effect which might be produced toward the desired object by a lesser combination of states, a convention which should include England, France, Germany, and the United States, with the concurrence of other states, both in Europe and on the American Continent, which this combination would assure, would be adequate to produce and maintain throughout the commercial world the relation between the two metals that such convention should adopt."

After the conference had held but thirteen sessions, upon the suggestion of the two governments of France and the United States, at whose instance it was convened, it adjourned to meet again April 12, 1882.

In submitting the proposition of adjournment, Monsieur De Normandie, a delegate of France, said: "We cannot disguise from ourselves that the observations just now submitted to you tend to nothing else than to establish, at least virtually, that nothing has been done here but an imperfect, useless, empty work."

No further action was taken by the convention at this session, and, so far as known, it did not reassemble at the date appointed; nor have the delegates from the United States ever submitted any report on the conference held.

Had the proposition submitted by Mr. Evarts on behalf of France and the United States been accepted, even as a unanimous expression of the opinion of the entire conference, it could hardly have received the sanction of the United States government, as it fixed the ratio between gold and silver at 1 to 15½. Another monetary conference called by the government of the United States met at Brussels, November 22, 1892. Twenty countries were represented. The delegates of the United States were Senators Wm. B. Allison and John P. Jones, Representative McCreary, and Messrs. Henry W. Cannon, E. Benjamin Andrews, and Edson H. Terrell. By the Secretary of State they were instructed that the main purpose sought by the government was to bring about a stable relation between gold and silver, but not through any plan which would place this government on a silver basis while European countries maintained the single gold standard. This stability of value was to be sought in the first instance by international bimetallism, or the unlimited coinage of gold and silver into money of full debt-paying power at a fixed ratio common to all the agreeing powers. Failing in that, they were to secure, if possible, some action on the part of European countries looking to a larger use of silver as currency in order to put an end to the further depreciation of that metal. In other words, the committee were to join with European nations in fixing a price for silver uniform and stable. As the conference was called by the United States, naturally the delegates from this country were expected to state the purpose of the meeting. This seems to have been somewhat embarrassing to them, but after a full consideration the delegates prepared a programme embodying the following resolution: "That in the opinion of this conference it is desirable that some measure should be found for increasing the use of silver in the currency of the nations." The subject of bimetallism, though not mentioned in the resolution, received some attention, enough to convince our delegates that the governments of Europe were not ready to adopt such a plan. Not one nation having a gold standard intimated any desire for a change. The delegates from Great Britain said, "Our faith is that of the school of monometallism, pure and simple; we do not admit that any other than the single gold standard would be applicable to our country." One from France said, "Why should France permit the free coinage of silver? I believe she alone possesses as much as all the states of Europe put together." The leading delegates from Germany said, "Germany, being satisfied with its monetary system, has no intention of modifying its basis." Austria-Hungary instructed its delegate to take no part in any discussion or vote. Holland instructed its delegate not to enter into any bimetallic union without the full participation of England; and so on through the list.

Our delegates soon concluded that if there were any chestnuts to pull from the fire they had mistaken the instruments to aid them. Of course there was nothing for them to do but to come home, and this they did after expressing their indebtedness to Belgium for its liberal provision for their comfort and convenience, with the understanding that the convention would be reconvened in May, 1893. This understanding may have mitigated the grief of parting, but it has thus far had no other effect, and it is doubtful if this country will ever again send its representatives abroad on such an errand.

The scheme of international bimetallism means, if anything, that all over the world, in every mart where silver is purchased, — and where is it not? — there shall be maintained every day a uniform price for that metal, measured by gold. Such a scheme is not without a parallel. The child's story book tells how it was agreed that every person in the world should cry "boo" at a certain fixed moment of time, that the man in the moon might hear it. No one person, however, believed that in so great an outcry his voice would be missed, and so when the moment arrived, only the deaf man from Borneo cried "boo;" and when the call is made for a uniform bid for silver throughout the world, the response will be of about the same unanimity, for the project has in it about the same amount of sense.

CHAPTER XXII.

THE TRADE DOLLAR.

AMONG the documents transmitted by the Secretary of the Treasury to Congress in 1870, with the draft of the bill proposing a revision of the coinage acts, was one by Prof. E. B. Elliot, of the Treasury Department, containing an elaborate discussion of the questions involved. In place of the then existing legal tender dollar he suggested the issue of a commercial dollar of nine-tenths fineness, and containing 25 grains of pure silver, being almost the exact equivalent of the silver contained in the old Spanish-Mexican pillar dollar, established in 1704 by a proclamation of Queen Anne, and declared to contain 386⅞ grains. The draft of the bill transmitted, however, contained no provision for such a coin, but it did provide for the coinage, on government account, of a silver dollar of 384 standard grains, being equal to the weight of one dollar of fractional coins, instead of the existing dollar of 412½ grains, and this provision remained in the bill as it first passed the Senate, January 9, 1871 — the suggestion of coining a piece for purely commercial purposes, and not for circulation, receiving little attention. The House failed to pass the bill in any form that session. Secretary Boutwell, however, in his annual report for 1872, renewed his recommendations for the passage of the coinage-revision bill, and suggested such alterations as would prohibit the coinage of silver as a general currency for the country, and also suggested that authority be given for the coinage of a silver dollar that should be as valuable as the Mexican dollar, to be furnished at cost; and he added that the Mexican dollar was used in trade with China, and was selling at a premium of eight per cent over the actual expense of coining.

In May, 1872, a new Congress having convened, the House took up the bill and passed it as originating in that body. The bill still provided for the coinage of a dollar of 384 standard grains. On January 7, 1873, Mr. Sherman reported the bill from the Senate finance committee, with certain amendments, of which by far the most important was the proposition to strike out the authority to coin a dollar for circulation, but in place of the one proposed to authorize a coin for only commercial purposes, to be coined for private parties at cost. He stated in explanation that this dollar had been adapted mainly for the benefit of the people of California and others engaged in trade with China. The amendment was accepted by the House, and the bill thus amended became a law February 12, 1873. The amendment was as follows: —

"That any owner of silver bullion may deposit the same at any mint, to be formed into bars, or into dollars of the weight of 420 grains troy, designated in this act as trade dollars . . . and the charges for converting standard silver into trade dollars; for melting and refining, when bullion is below standard; for toughening, when metals are contained in it which render it unfit for coinage; for copper used for alloy, when the bullion is above standard; for separating the gold and silver, when these metals exist together in the bullion; and for the preparation of bars, shall be fixed from time to time by the Director (of the Mint), with the concurrence of the Secretary of the Treasury, so as to equal, but not exceed, in their judgment, the actual average cost to each mint and assay office, of the material, labor, wastage, and use of machinery employed in each of the cases aforementioned."

The name of the coin, and the manner in which it was to be issued, confirmed the oft-repeated assertions of its friends, that the coin was for commercial purposes only, and not intended for circulation. Through what appears to be an oversight, however, another section of the same law, in declaring what should be the silver coins of the United States, included the trade dollar, and made that coin, like other silver coins, a legal tender for any amount not exceeding five dollars in any one payment.

Immediately upon the passage of the act, designs for the new coin were prepared and accepted. On the one side was to be a left-handed view of the goddess of liberty, and on the other side the name of the coin, with the announcement that the piece contained 420 grains of silver nine-tenths fine, surrounded with the words "THE UNITED STATES OF AMERICA." Arrangements for its coinage being concluded, holders of silver bullion were notified that, upon presentation of it at the United States Mint in either Philadelphia or San Francisco, they could obtain these coins in return, upon additional payment of $1\frac{1}{4}$ cents for each piece, the estimated cost of manufacture.

The certificate the coin bore as to its weight and fineness was accepted in China and Japan without farther assaying or weighing of the metal, and the form of the metal being adapted for circulation, the coin created a new market for silver, and readily sold at a considerable advance above other forms of silver bullion. As the coin would bring for exportation more than a dollar in gold, there was no object in putting it into circulation in this country. But owing to the depreciation in the value of silver, which soon followed, it became of less value than the paper dollar, and eventually less than that of the gold dollar.

The holders of bullion then found it more profitable to put the coin into circulation in this country than to export it, and suddenly, as if by magic, the coins appeared in all parts of the country, to the surprise of nearly everybody, as even the authority for its coinage was not generally known. It soon came into competition with the other dollar authorized by the same act, and holders were perplexed beyond measure to understand why the former coin, having $7\frac{1}{2}$ grains more of silver in it than had the latter, should be a legal tender for five dollars only, while the latter was an unlimited tender in the payment of all debts. The confusion was increased when they ascertained that the government sold the former in any amount, with only cost of coinage added, while it was restricted in the coinage of the latter, and compelled to sell it at its face value in gold, regardless of the price of silver bullion. Appeals for information concerning this financial puzzle came to the Treasury from all parts of the country, not unfrequently accompanied by a statement that the information was desired to settle a wager as to the relative worth of the two coins. A full explanation was embodied in one reply, and to save labor this reply was printed, and thereafter sent to all inquirers. The letter was dated September 1, 1878, and was signed by the Secretary. The following extract fully explains the character and circulation of the coin: —

"As its name indicates, the purpose of this coin was for *trade*, not for circulation, though by classifying it with other silver coins, the law made it a legal tender to the amount of five (5) dollars in any one payment.

"At the time of the passage of the act the actual value of this dollar, including the charge of $1\frac{1}{4}$ cents for coinage, was a little more than $1.04 in gold.

"Under such circumstances there could be no object for the owner to put the coins into circulation, and consequently they were exported mostly to China, where, from lack of a circulating medium, these pieces, convenient in size, and bearing the guaranty of a great government as to their weight and fineness, obtained an extensive circulation, and created a market for the silver of the Pacific States, as intended by the act.

"After a few months, however, an unforeseen depreciation in the value of silver bullion occurred; and in the early part of 1876 this depreciation reached such a point that one dollar in gold would purchase more than the necessary amount of silver for a trade dollar, and pay for its coinage.

"Under such conditions, dealers in bullion found a profit in putting trade dollars into circulation at par in the Pacific States, where the currency was upon a gold basis; but the coin being a legal tender for only five (5) dollars, its circulation was necessarily limited in amount as well as restricted in locality.

"The people of the Pacific States, however, objected to its use at all for circulation, and the attention of Congress having been called to the matter, on the 8th of May, 1876, Hon. Samuel J. Randall of Pennsylvania introduced into the House a bill, the third section of which repealed the legal tender quality of these coins.

"On the 10th of June following, Hon. S. S. Cox of New York reported the measure to the House, urging its adoption.

"No objection was raised, and it became a law July 22, 1876, without modification or an opposing voice or vote in either House, and is as follows:—

"'That the trade dollar shall not hereafter be a legal tender; and the Secretary of the Treasury is hereby authorized to limit, from time to time, the coinage thereof to such an amount as he may deem sufficient to meet the export demand for the same.'

"Up to that time (excepting a few days), and for several months thereafter, the trade dollar cost more than a paper-currency dollar, and consequently none of the coins got into circulation in other than the Pacific States.

"Owing to the appreciation of the paper currency, however, in the fall of 1877, the trade dollar became of less value than the paper dollar; and in December of that year a large number of them were put into circulation, at their face value, at a profit to the owners of the bullion."

"Apprehensive of such misuse of the coins, on the 15th of October in that year I ordered the discontinuance of their coinage at the mint at Philadelphia, and four days later at the other mints.* Meanwhile the Department, in reply to numerous inquiries, had uniformly stated that the trade dollar possessed only a commercial value, depending upon the price of silver bullion.

"It will be seen that the coins were put into circulation months after the passage of the act taking from them their legal tender character, and mainly after their coinage had ceased.

"But in their use as money, the Department has never had any interest or derived any profit. For the expense of their coinage the owners of the bullion reimbursed the government, and this ended the connection of the government with the transaction. At no time and on no account have they

---

* These orders were subsequently modified to permit a limited amount to be coined for exportation only.

ever been received, or paid out, by the Treasury; and it is a cause of regret that so many of our people should have accepted them at their face value, thus enabling their owners to put them into circulation at a considerable profit.

"Under date of July 25, 1878, the Director of the Mint published tables from which the value of these coins can be ascertained, and the terms on which they are received at the mints. He does not advise any one to dispose of them at such rates. The law under which the Department buys bullion with which to coin the standard silver dollar, requires the same to be bought at the market price, and it can purchase trade dollars only as bullion. Possibly in time these coins will find a ready market in China at nearly or quite their face value, for circulation as coin."

The repeal of the law giving this coin a legal tender quality only added to the mystery of its existence. Congress could but recognize the illogical position the coin occupied in the currency of the country. Although containing more silver than the standard dollar, it would not be received in payment of public dues, nor could the holder lawfully pay with it any private debt.

There were coined 35,965,924 of these pieces, of which about 6,000,000 probably remained in this country. To finally dispose of the troublesome coins the House of Representatives in 1884 passed an act authorizing their redemption at par in gold, and directing their recoinage into standard dollars. This would doubtless have relieved the circulation of the country from their undesired presence; but the plan offered to foreign holders of these coins ten per cent more than would be paid to holders of silver bullion in other forms, and such a percentage of profit would hardly fail to bring back to the country all the trade dollars then in existence. And after settling with foreign holders, at a profit to them of ten per cent, the government proposed to take out a large per cent of the silver for itself, and then to sell the coins again to the public at par in gold! The act never passed the Senate.

Finally Congress in 1887 authorized the exchange of these pieces for standard dollars, and in this way there have been received at the mint 7,689,036 of them, which, though containing more silver than the standard dollar, were overrated as bullion, thus imposing a loss upon the government.

The purpose and the result of the issue of this coin afford but another example of the fallacy of legislative acts to improve upon natural commercial laws. Authorized as an avowed agency to assist mining industries, the coin at first filled its mission satisfactorily, but events which legislators could not foresee completely changed its original character and object, and brought to its holders loss, annoyance, and confusion. The government should never have embarked in the enterprise. It departed from its proper functions to legislate in the interests of a few persons, with the result we have seen. It might as well upon a proper consideration have placed its stamp upon the ends of a pork-barrel for the pork-packer in Chicago, certifying that the barrel contained the lawful amount and quality of mess pork. To complete the illustration, it might then declare the barrel to be a legal tender within a prescribed limit!

CHAPTER XXIII.

OTHER MONEYS.

MINOR COINS. The act of April 2, 1792, authorized the coinage of copper cent and half-cent pieces, of 264 and 132 grains respectively. These pieces were not legal tender for any amount or made redeemable upon any terms. To those who wished for them, they were sold at the mints at their face value for gold or silver. Consequently no greater amount got into circulation than was required for convenience in making change, for which purpose they were readily accepted. In the following year the weight of the cent piece was reduced to 208 grains; in 1796, to 168 grains, the half-cent suffering a corresponding reduction. The coinage of both pieces was discontinued by law in 1857, to which time they were the only authorized coins in circulation of less value than the silver half-dime.

At the same time, to take the place of these worthy coins, a so-called nickel cent was authorized, to weigh 72 grains, and to be composed of 88 per cent copper and 12 per cent nickel. This piece was smaller than its predecessor and less cumbersome, but was apt to be mistaken for the gold quarter-eagle, being of nearly the same diameter and thickness. It had no legal tender quality, and was not redeemable in any other money; but it answered the purpose for which it was coined as well, but no better, than its predecessor.

By the act of April 22, 1864, the coinage of this nickel cent was prohibited, and in its place one and two cent bronze pieces were authorized, to weigh respectively 48 and 96 grains, to be composed of 95 per cent copper and 5 per cent tin and zinc, and to be a legal tender in any payment for 10 cents and 20 cents respectively. Their issue was prohibited by the act of February 12, 1873.

By the act of March 3, 1865, a three cent nickel piece was authorized, to weigh 30 grains, to be composed of 75 per cent copper and 25 per cent nickel, and to be a legal tender in any payment to the amount of 60 cents. The same act reduced the legal tender limit of the one and two cent coins to four cents.

By the act of May 16, 1866, a five cent nickel piece was authorized, to weigh 77.16 grains, to be composed of 75 per cent copper and 25 per cent nickel, to be a legal tender in any payment to the amount of one dollar, and to be redeemed by the Treasury in national currency when presented in sums of one hundred dollars.

By the act of March 3, 1871, the redemption in lawful money of all the above coins is provided for when presented in sums of twenty dollars.

It is doubtful if any case has arisen in which any advantage has arisen from the legal tender quality of these coins, and no harm or good has therefore come from this endowment. The coins were however designed only for the convenience of the public in "making change," and only this purpose was served until they were made redeemable in lawful money. Taking advantage of that provision, banks, street-car companies, bake-shops, and others receiving large amounts of minor coins have turned these coins into the Treasury in exchange for lawful money; and the Treasury has been compelled thus to receive them and then to reissue them to persons needing them, thus throwing upon the government a labor and expense which should be borne by the parties in interest.

FRACTIONAL SILVER. Half-dollar, quarter-dollar, dime, and half-dime pieces were authorized by the act of April 2, 1792. They were of the same fineness as the dollar, and of relative weight. They were a full legal tender in payment of debts, and their coinage continued after 1809, when the coinage of the dollar ceased; but they were mainly exported, depreciated paper constituting the circulating medium of the country.

Upon the reduction in the weight of gold coins in 1837, silver coins were undervalued, and the country consequently left without any silver for change, a want partly supplied by worn Mexican pieces. To correct this evil the act of February 21, 1853, provided that the weight of these fractional pieces should be reduced, so that one dollar in value should weigh 384 grains, instead of 412½, making a dollar worth considerably less than one dollar in gold, an intentional over-valuation, in order that the pieces might not be melted down or exported. The pieces were then no longer coined for depositors, but on government account, being issued in exchange for gold, par for par, the profit in the coinage being turned into the public treasury. They were also made a legal tender only for sums not exceeding five dollars. Subsequently a three-cent piece and a twenty-cent piece were authorized, but the authority for their issue has been discontinued.

By an act approved June 9, 1879, the redemption in lawful money of the silver coins of smaller denominations than one dollar was authorized, and the coins made a legal tender for all sums not exceeding ten dollars. Unexpected results followed the provision for redeeming these coins. It was supposed that the excess likely to be presented for that purpose would be insignificant; and, could the redemption have been limited to the coins then in the country, such would have been the result.

But while the country was using fractional paper currency the fractional silver had been largely exported to Canada and the South American States, in which places it circulated at its bullion value. As soon as the government offered to redeem the coins at par in gold or its equivalent, the holders in those countries lost no time in sending in their coins for redemption, realizing from the exchange a profit of not less than 25 per cent. The amount of about $28,000,000 of these coins was redeemed, of which a great amount still remains in the Treasury vaults.

Not only has the government been thus overreached, but, as in the case of the minor coins, the public Treasury has become a distributing agent, but working in this case for the benefit of the banks, dime museums, and travelling shows in redeeming and redistributing these coins. As the coins are convertible at sight into full legal tender money, the limit of their legal tender quality becomes of no importance.

CLEARING-HOUSE CERTIFICATES. By the act of June 8, 1873, the Treasury was authorized to receive United States notes on deposit from national banks in sums of not less than ten thousand dollars, and to issue certificates therefor, receivable at the clearing-house in payment of balances, the certificates to be payable on demand, and no expansion or contraction of the currency to arise from the transaction. Under this authority banks employ the public Treasury to keep them in notes of denominations which may suit their convenience, turning into the Sub-Treasury one day worn notes of undesirable denominations, obtaining certificates therefor to be redeemed the next day in new notes of desired denominations, compelling the Sub-Treasury offices to make the exchange in Washington, at the expense of the government. No other advantage in the plan has yet become evident.

SILVER CERTIFICATES. These certificates, heretofore mentioned, are issued upon deposits of silver dollars held in the Treasury for their redemption upon presentation. These are receivable by the government for any public dues, but are not a legal tender for private debts. The authority for their issue was repealed November 1, 1893, at which time there had been issued about $250,000,000.

GOLD CERTIFICATES. These certificates are issued upon the deposits of gold in the Treasury, and are redeemable in gold at sight. They are receivable by the government only for customs dues, and are not a legal tender for private debts.

The Treasury has, without authority of law, recognized them as lawful reserves for national banks; and for this purpose they are ever in demand. In any stringency, gold can be obtained for them at sight, and the banks can thus have available gold without cumbering their vaults with the heavy metal, the government kindly performing that function for them. Excepting for the resumption fund of $100,000,000, the Treasury can issue certificates for any gold it owns.

TREASURY NOTES. Under the act of July 14, 1890, the Secretary of the Treasury was directed to purchase from time to time 4,500,000 ounces of pure silver each month at the market price, and to issue in payment of such purchases Treasury notes, to be a legal tender in payment of all debts public and private, except otherwise expressly stipulated in the contract, to be redeemable in either gold or silver coin at the discretion of the Secretary, and when redeemed to be reissued. The authority for the issue of these notes was repealed November 1, 1893, at which time there had been issued $155,931,002.

CHAPTER XXIV.

THE PAR OF EXCHANGE.

By the rating of the British mint in 1707 the pound sterling silver was valued at 4.44$\frac{4}{9}$ Spanish silver dollars, as they were then current in the American colonies. At that time the dollar contained 386$\frac{1}{8}$ grains of pure silver. Subsequent reductions were made in the legal weight of this piece, until the coinage act of 1792 fixed the weight at 371$\frac{1}{4}$ grains of such silver, at which it has since remained.

The silver pound sterling, which in 1707 contained 1719.4 grains of pure silver, remained unchanged until 1816, when Great Britain demonetized silver, and declared in effect that the pound sterling or the sovereign should consist of 113+ grains of pure gold. Of course the value of this pound expressed in silver dollars would thereafter vary in accordance with the unceasing fluctuations in the relative commercial value of the two metals. But an official proclamation had declared the pound sterling equal to \$4.44$\frac{4}{9}$; and in all commercial dealings this rating continued to be nominally recognized until 1834, although the amount in dollars, where pounds were called for, would be calculated at an entirely different rate, and at a rate which changed from day to day.

In 1834 the gold dollar became the unit of value in the United States, and that unit bore fixed relation to the unit of value in Great Britain, both being of the same metal, but the pound sterling still continued to be rated at 4.44\frac{4}{9}$. In 1837 the amount of pure gold in the dollar was fixed at 23.22 grains. The number of these dollars in a pound sterling would therefore be 4.8665, or in other words the value of the pound was $4.8665, being 9½ per cent above the recognized value of 4.44\frac{4}{9}$.

Until January 1, 1873, the valuation of the pound sterling at 4.44\frac{4}{9}$ continued to find place in all transactions involving the currencies of the two countries. The school arithmetics taught the value of a pound sterling to be 4.44\frac{4}{9}$, but that the true "par of exchange" was found in this country by adding to that value 9½ per cent of itself, and that the commercial value would then be found by adding to or subtracting from this result the small percentage fixed by dealers, varying from time to time according to the rates of insurance, interest, and transportation, and the demand for drafts on London payable in pounds sterling. Thus for 166 years the value of the pound sterling was estimated in accordance with the proclamation issued by Queen Anne in 1707, although meanwhile the silver dollar had twice been changed in weight, and both dollar and pound had been changed from silver to gold.

This undervaluation of the pound sterling caused in commercial transactions only an inconvenience of calculation; nobody gained anything by it, or lost anything except additional time consumed in arithmetical calculations.

In computing duties on imported goods from England levied at a certain percentage upon their value at the place of shipment, customs officers, however, found that, reckoning the pound sterling at 4.44\frac{4}{9}$, the government was not obtaining the revenue which the law evidently contemplated, and at the same time was discriminating in favor of England as against other nations sending their goods to this country.

In 1842 Congress imposed a high tariff on imported goods, and, with a view of equalizing rates among the different countries from which the goods came, determined to readjust the value of the pound sterling, known to be underrated. For this purpose an English sovereign was tested at the mint, and upon the result of the test Congress declared the value of that piece to be $4.84. This erroneous rating, evidently based upon the weight of a piece somewhat worn, gave more duties to the government, more protection to "infant industries," and to the importer of dutiable goods from England another rating of the pound to confuse his reckonings.

To relieve the importers and others in any way interested in foreign exchanges, Congress in 1872 enacted a law declaring that the value of foreign coins, as expressed in the money of account of the United States, should be that of the pure metal of such coin of standard value, and that the standard coins in circulation of the various nations of the world should be estimated annually by the Director of the Mint, and proclaimed on the first day of January, by the Secretary of the Treasury; and that in all payments to or by the Treasury, where it became necessary to compute the value of the pound sterling, such pound should be deemed equal to $4.8665, and the same value should apply in appraising merchandise imported where the value was expressed in pounds or sovereigns, and that this valuation should be the par of exchange between the United States and Great Britain.

The first proclamation of value of foreign coins was issued by the Secretary, January 1, 1873, and immediately thereafter quotations of sterling exchange were based upon the new value of the pound.

This value was found by dividing the number of grains of pure gold in a standard sovereign by the number of such grains in a standard dollar, — a process so simple that the delay of forty years in reaching the result seems unaccountable.

England, however, had been in this matter equally as dilatory as the United States. In all transactions involving dollars, the pound was rated at $4.44⅘, and the result corrected by the percentage necessary to obtain the true value. Published quotations of the value of American securities in London assumed that undervaluation of the pound as the correct par of exchange; and to the extent of the undervaluation they were misleading, except to the comparatively few who knew of the error so persistently maintained.

In 1873 the Secretary of the Treasury communicated with the proper representative of the Stock Exchange in London, advising him of the reform in this country, by which the pound sterling had come to be reckoned and quoted at its true value, and suggested that a corresponding change be made in the usage of the London Stock Exchange, that the value of American securities might be correctly published in that city.

The matter was favorably presented to the Exchange, but it met with little favor. The error was so well understood, it was alleged, that no change was necessary or desirable; but finally, in the nature of a compromise, the Exchange adopted $5 as the value of the sovereign, upon which par future quotations of American securities would be published, and peremptorily closed the discussion, perhaps fearing an inquiry as to what process of reasoning had been used to obtain the result.

To ascertain the true value in London of securities calling for dollars, the published quotations of the Stock Exchange in that city must now be reduced in the ratio of 500 to 486.65; but, to obtain the commercial value of such securities, the current exchange value of the pound should be substituted in place of its legal value.

CHAPTER XXV.

CONCLUSION.

That any question as to the kind or amount of money to be employed as a circulating medium in any country should ever find its way to the halls of legislation or to a political caucus cannot but be regretted. Money was introduced by the commercial world exclusively for its own convenience, and as long as it remains so there nothing is heard of an insufficient supply, of bimetallism, seigniorage, monetary conventions, legal tender, Gresham's law, subsidiary coins, trade dollars, demonetization of silver, or of the dreaded gold bug. Money left to itself performs its duty silently, asking for no favors, but bestowing blessings on all alike. It is only when taken out of the channels of trade to be reformed and improved by legislation that it stirs up strife or engenders ridicule.

This country has not hesitated to juggle with its currency at any time, as if in some way it was a wealth-giving power instead of only a machine for effecting exchanges, or, more accurately speaking, only the oil which lubricates the machine; and with what result? The muse of history to-day stands with her arms akimbo, laughing at our puerile efforts to make the shells of ocean, the products of the field, and paper promises to pay, with no time specified, do the work of a circulating medium by virtue of an act of Congress; at our ceaseless prating for eighty years of our double standard, gold and silver, the latest and greatest gift to mankind, by which both metals circulated on equal terms, and then at our anathemas upon suddenly discovering that we had no double standard and never did have, except on the pages of the statute; at our making worn Spanish coins of a dollar or less denomination of full debt-paying power, by which our own silver coins fresh and plump from the mint were driven from use, leaving us only "pillar pieces" of halves and quarters and eighths worn so thin that upon the visit of a country pedler the sharpest eyes of the household were called in to determine whether or not the pillars on the coin were visible, for if not, or if some one had scratched an X on it, the quarter shrunk to twenty cents, the eighth to ten cents; at our employment of depreciated legal tender notes to meet the expenses of the war, and to "float the loans" by which our national debt was doubled with no gain to the government, which could at any time have had coin by asking for it, and keeping out of competition disreputable associates who drove it away; at our coinage of a trade dollar to help the producers of silver find a market for their product, and at our final purchase of the pieces at above the market rate to avoid further embarrassing explanations; at the purchase of silver bullion to be stowed away under ground while upon it certificates were issued ostensibly to make money easy, but in fact hastening and intensifying a panic to check which their further issue was prohibited, but not until the silver on hand had a market value of $136,000,000 less than it cost; and at our accumulating a reserve of $100,000,000 in gold coin with which to maintain at par $346,000,000 of United States notes, then making $500,000,000 silver certificates or notes also redeemable therefrom, and then using the reserve to pay current expenses, and all in the name of the law.

There is danger that the laugh which has come circling down to us from colonial days will continue another generation. The unremitting interference of political with economical laws has borne its fruit. Jack Cade is abroad in the land, promising his followers that when he is king seven halfpenny loaves of bread shall be sold for a penny to help the working man, and at the same time for a sixpence to keep up the price of wheat; that all people shall be clad in one livery; that the three-hooped pot shall have ten hoops; that the city conduit shall run nothing but red wine; and that he will have five-shilling wheat and six-penny cotton, to equalize things in his kingdom. The magic wand which is to usher in this material millennium is of legislative make, and known as the free coinage of silver at a ratio to gold of 16 to 1. To be sure the present ratio is nearer 30 to 1, but that is a matter of no moment. Congress can regulate that. The advocates of free silver must be presumed to know that legislation never did fix prices of commodities and never will. Congress attempted once to fix the price of gold, but its utter failure to accomplish such a purpose is recounted on the pages of this volume. In the so-called bimetallism silver will be worth in the market precisely what the world of commerce may determine, with no reference to our wishes or any act of Congress; and with the restoration of silver to free coinage for depositors at 16 to 1 we may expect with certainty to see all gold disappear from circulation, a loss at once of about $500,000,000; to see the silver in circulation shrink in our hands to its commercial value, about one-half its present value, about $300,000,000 loss to circulation, or $800,000,000 in all at the outset, to say nothing in the shrinkage of United States and national bank notes, which will then be redeemable at par in silver dollars. To restore our metallic circulation to its present value would take all our mints coining silver at their full capacity more than twenty years, and in the end what would the country gain? It would have a value standard about one-half the size of the one displaced, a matter of trifling moment in current transactions. The franc, one-fifth of a dollar, proves just as satisfactory a standard as the pound, nearly five dollars. All is, one must have more francs to make his purchases. It is the getting to a new basis that will invite the whirlwind in our business, and the same would be the result under like conditions whether going from gold to silver or silver to gold. Let it be once understood that the present silver dollar is to become the standard of value in this country, and more than $2,000,000,000 of our securities held abroad will be sold out at once at any sacrifice. Municipalities and corporations wishing to sell bonds will find no purchasers. Depositors in savings banks will demand a return of their money before the depreciated dollar can come into use, and $1,700,000,000 savings now used in maintaining industries will be withdrawn to be hoarded against the coming storm, and everywhere financial disaster will raise its head and stalk through the land, closing our factories, putting out the fire in our furnaces, encouraging and stimulating strife and riots. There is no escaping the result. If the advocates of free silver do not mean a repudiation of credit, there is no excuse for their existence.

The employment of either silver or gold is only a question of convenience. There is no sentiment in it. To change from one to another, differing greatly in power, will at any time produce commotion and injury, and should not be attempted unless necessary for national existence. We have to-day a gold standard, but silver in circulation, maintained at a gold valuation by the pledged resources of the country, exceeding the amount of gold. The system may not be a model one, but under it both metals are employed with reasonable equality, and, if possible, the country should be given a rest and money taken from politics, where it never belonged, and left to the care of the commercial world, where it will find a congenial home and pleasant employment.

INDEX.

	PAGE
Argale, Governor	6
Bancroft on colonial metallic currency	13
Bank circulation in 1861	108
Bank issues, mania for	45, 47
Barter	5
Benton, Thomas H., against Hamilton, 41; denounces equalization of gold and silver	162, 173, 175
Biddle, Charles, on American wealth in Revolution	30
Bill suppressing gambling in gold	182
Bills of Credit prohibited	42
"Black Friday"	169
Bland Silver Bill, the	229
Boutwell, Secretary of Treasury	134
Bristow, Secretary of Treasury	149
Bronson on colonial legal tender	18
Buccaneers, the	7
Bull Run, effects of	71
Bureau of Engraving and Printing organized	92
Certificates	271, 272
Chase, Salmon P., Secretary of Treasury, 68, 70, 73, 74, 76, 79, 83, 90, 91, 94, 99, 113, 116, 121, 182	
"Cheap Money"	viii
Clearing House Certificates	271
Coinage act of 1792, 171; of 1873	193, 217
Coins, minor (one-cent to five-cent pieces)	267
Collamer, of Vermont, declares legal tender act unconstitutional, 85; opposes national banks	118
Colonies, mistaken financial policy of	32
Commodities, relative prices of	197
Comptroller of Currency, authorized and appointed	119

(287)

INDEX.

	PAGE
Confusion in early coinage	9
Conger Bill, the	232
Congress adopts Spanish dollar as unit of value	35
Congress and the circulating medium	28
Conkling, Roscoe, opposes legal tender act	79
Connecticut paper money	18
Constitution of United States, framed, 37; adopted	37
Contraction of national issues	126, 129, 134
Corn a legal tender	5
Cox, S. S., advocates the repeal of the trade dollar act	262
Crash of 1809, 44; of 1814, 46; of 1818, 47; of 1837, 50; of 1841, 66; of 1857, 51; of 1861, 74; of 1869, 190; of 1873, 136; of 1893, 233	
Currency, depreciation of, in 1814	46
Dallas, Secretary of Treasury	55, 57
Darien, Ga., Bank of	48
Depletion of the Treasury	xiv
Depreciation of early paper money	20
Dexter, Jr., Andrew	43
"Dollar of our Daddies," the	226
Dollar, subdivisions of	35
Double standard of values first established in U.S.	22
Eagle, gold, coinage of	35
Edward III., King of England	1
Elizabeth, Queen	2
England, single standard of	173
England, standard pound of	1
Exchange, rates of	274, 279
Farmers' Exchange Bank of Gloucester, R.I.	43, 44
Fessenden, chairman Committee on Finance	83, 84
Fractional silver coins	269
Franklin, Benjamin, on paper money	18
Free silver, dangers of	284
Free silver, discontinued	222
Gold and silver, value of	vii
Gold as a monetary standard	196
Gold certificates, issued, 155; character of	272

	PAGE
Gold dollar the unit of value	176
Gold fluctuations	75, 179, 183, 189
Gold speculation	186, 188
Grant, President, on silver	145

"Halifax Award," the 151
Hamilton, Alexander, Secretary of Treasury, 38; authorizes the
    mint, 39; recommends a national bank 40
Harrington, Assistant Secretary of Treasury 71
Hen-yard productions of U.S. xviii
Hepburn case, the 158, 160, 162, 163
Hooper, of Massachusetts, advocates national banks 117

Illinois silver legislation 227

"Jack Cade" theories 282
Jefferson, Thomas, recommends dollar subdivisions, 36; on
    revolutionary currency, 3–6, 27; on cost of Revolution . . . 32
Jevons, Professor, anecdote iv

Land values, rise in 49
Latin Union, the 220, 235
Legal-tender Act . . . . xxi, 78, 81, 83, 85, 87, 88, 90
Legal-tender currency xix
Legal-tender notes 96, 98, 103, 107, 108, 110, 157, 165
Lincoln, Abraham, inauguration of 68
"London Times," on American affairs 72
Louisburg, capture of 20
Lovejoy, of Illinois, opposes legal-tender act 80

Madison, James, silver letter of 204
Maryland, coinage in 10
Maryland dollar 12
Massachusetts, coinage in 8
Massachusetts, colony of, early laws 4, 8
Massachusetts grants bank charter 42
Massachusetts paper money 14
Massachusetts' penalty for failure to redeem bills 45
McCulloch, Hugh, Secretary of Treasury 126
Mexican War "squeeze" 51

INDEX.

	PAGE
Mint at Boston established in 1652	8
Mint, U.S., establishment of suggested, 34; authorized, 39; effected	214
Monetary Conference of 1878, 236; of 1881, 242; of 1882, 252; of 1892	253
Money cost of American revolution	32
Money cost of Civil war	xx
Money, man's best friend	x
Money most plentiful where commodities are cheapest	viii
Money, value of	280
Morrill, of Vermont, opposes legal-tender act, 79; secretary of treasury	149
Morris, Robert, recommendations as Superintendent of Finance,	33, 34, 36
"Moving the crops"	185, 188
National Bank recommended by Dallas	55
National Bank Charter, renewal refused	45
National Banking system recommended, 113; opposed, 117; act passed, 119; opposition disappears	125
Nevada silver yield	220
New Jersey dollar	12
New Jersey, petition of 1834	210
New York dollar	12
New York guards against suspension of specie payments	52
New York "Tribune" on Spaulding bill	76
Niles's "Register" on U.S. Bank	62
North Carolina dollar	12
Ohio Life and Trust Company, failure of	51
One to fifteen ratio asserted by Hamilton, 39; established	172, 203
"One to sixteen," a party cry, 207; bill establishing this ratio	208
Panics, *see* Crash.	
"Paper Devils," the	79
Paper money in colonies	17, 19, 21
Patriotism in finance	71
Peag, 3; deterioration of	4
Pennsylvania dollar	12
Pennsylvania grants bank charters in 1814	45

INDEX. 291

	PAGE
Pennsylvania paper money	17
Philadelphia's "golden age"	47
Prices of commodities	viii
Prosperity of United States, 1857–1861	67

Ratios of silver to gold, fixing the 283
Reagen amendment, the 225
Remonetization demanded 228, 229, 232, 233
Reserve in Treasury, treatment of 154
Revolutionary paper money, 24; value of 29
Rhode Island, action respecting money 13
Rhode Island financial " contrivances " 42
Rhode Island paper money 15
Richardson, Secretary, directions of 145

Sauerbeck, Augustus, on price of commodities 196
Seville dollar, the 38
Shell currency 3
Sherman Act, the 233
Sherman, John, favors legal-tender act, 85; favors national bank-
    ing system, 118; favors resumption of specie payment, 146;
    secretary of treasury 93, 149, 150, 151, 232
Shilling of colonial days in America 8, 11
Shilling of England 2, 8
Silver certificates 272
Silver dollar, the 201
Silver, fluctuations in 202, 205, 219
Silver product of U.S., value of xviii
Society Islands, anecdote of v
South Carolina dollar 12
Spanish pillar dollar 11, 13, 34, 35, 201, 256
Spaulding bill, the 76
Specie equivalent collected during Civil war 32
Specie resumption in 1818, 48; in 1836, 50; in 1876, 146, 152;
    in 1879 195
State banks in 1861, 111; poor condition of, 122; (in 1865) 126
Stevens, of Pennsylvania, favors legal-tender act, 82; opposes
    amendments, 88; bill for ways and means 95
Sub-treasury act of 1846 209

INDEX.

	PAGE
Sumner, Charles, favors legal-tender act	86
Supreme Court decisions	159, 164, 166, 169

Tariff, Protective, of 1840 51
Tight money market ix
Tobacco currency in Virginia 11
Trade dollar, the 256, 259, 262, 264, 265
Treasury notes authorized 53
Treasury notes of 1861, 65, 68, 69, 70, 72, 73, 78, 83, 84, 88, 92, 96, 116, 127; (of 1874), 140; (of 1890) 273
Treasury sales of gold 184, 185, 186
True money iii

United States Bank authorized, 60; established, 60; criticised, 62; relief of, 63; re-charter vetoed, 64; closed, 65; death of . . . 66
United States, money in xi

Value of dollar fixed by Congress 35
Vanderbilt, the railway king iv

"Wild-cat" currency 49
Winthrop, Governor 13

Zelie, Mlle., anecdote of iv

www.ingramcontent.com/pod-product-compliance
Lightning Source LLC
Chambersburg PA
CBHW030810230426
43667CB00008B/1145